The Goats of Wrath and Other Stories:

A Peace Corps Family's Adventures in Thailand, 1972-1975

To my good neighbor, Donna, who is our neighborhood lifeline. Hope you enjoy my book. Stay Well!

Pat

THE GOATS OF WRATH

AND OTHER STORIES

A PEACE CORPS FAMILY'S
ADVENTURES IN THAILAND,
1972–1975

PATRICIA LIDRICH

INKWATER PRESS

Copyright © 2017 by Patricia Lidrich.

Cover and interior design by Michael Ebert.

Thai Style Ancient Roof and Sky in the Temple Thailand © Yongkiet. DreamsTime.com.
Serow (Mountain Goat Capricornis sumatraensis) stand on rock at Chiangrai, Thailand © stockdevil. DreamsTime.com.
Goat Icon © Freepik. Flaticon.com.

All rights reserved. No part of this book may be reproduced or transmitted in any form or by any means whatsoever, including photocopying, recording or by any information storage and retrieval system, without written permission from the publisher and/or author. The views and opinions expressed in this book are those of the author(s) and do not necessarily reflect those of the publisher, and the publisher hereby disclaims any responsibility for them. Neither is the publisher responsible for the content or accuracy of the information provided in this document. Contact Inkwater Press at inkwater.com. 503.968.6777

Publisher: Inkwater Press | www.inkwaterpress.com

Paperback
ISBN-13 978-1-62901-364-0 | ISBN-10 1-62901-364-1

Kindle
ISBN-13 978-1-62901-365-7 | ISBN-10 1-62901-365-X

Printed in the U.S.A.

1 3 5 7 9 10 8 6 4 2

For my dear sons, Nathan and Matthew.

Contents

Acknowledgements...ix
Introduction..xi
1. First Impressions..1
2. American Housekeeping, Thai Style..............................9
3. Culture Conundrums...23
4. The Blind Leading the Blind......................................31
5. Blind School Postscript...43
6. Motorcycle Mama..47
7. Revolution...57
8. The Goats of Wrath...63
9. Hijacked in Hong Kong...73
10. Thai Riverboat Adventure..79
11. A Trip Back in Time...93
12. Remembrances..109
Photographs...117
About the Author...121

Acknowledgements

How could I possibly remember events that happened over 40 years ago? Many of these adventures I could never forget! But I also mined long-forgotten details from notes I'd taken at the time, and a couple of articles I wrote shortly after we returned to the U.S. The letters that I sent home every week to my parents, Dr. and Mrs. Ted Dennis, were quite invaluable. Google certainly came in handy at times.

I'd like readers to know that I put Thai words into phonetic English, to the best of my ability. You see, the Thai language uses a completely different alphabet.

My appreciation is extended to the following people:

My writing teacher, Eva Jane Gibson, for her instruction, suggestions, and encouragement.

My classmates for their help and support.

My friend Marilyn Matteson for her patient first editing.

My husband, Neal, for painstakingly preparing the manuscript and the photos for the publishing company. I want to also thank him for his continuous love and devotion.

My other family members and friends for cheering me on.

My Thai, European, and American friends for helping us learn Thai culture and language and, at times, sharing in our adventures.

Introduction

I didn't want to go. I dreaded the prospect.

The year was 1971. My family and I had moved to the little town of Gilbert, Iowa. My parents and cousins lived about twenty miles away. With the help of Professor Meglitsch at Drake University in Des Moines, my husband had secured a position as a laboratory instructor at Iowa State University.

He had earned a doctorate in zoology three years before and taught two years at a small college in Orange, California. Unfortunately, he was laid off, and couldn't find a similar appointment anywhere. However, we considered ourselves fortunate that he was working at all.

Joe, however, longed to teach regular classes in college again. And, lo and behold, he found the Peace Corps accepted families.

I didn't want to go. I dreaded the prospect.

My husband had always been very persuasive, so when my parents agreed to babysit for our three-year-old twins, Matthew and Nathan, whom we called Mattie and Nate, I accompanied him to interviews in Philadelphia. These lasted several days, and in the end, we signed contracts to teach in Chiang Mai, Thailand. Joe would have a professorship in biology, and I would teach half-time at a school for blind students. While I was working, our children could attend a nursery school taught by a German woman.

At that time, the Vietnam War raged. My parents argued against going. Joe cooed, "It will make me so happy, Tricia!" We left in the spring of 1972.

I didn't really want to go. I dreaded the prospect. And yet, once we made that decision, I was determined to soldier on.

These stories tell about our lives in Thailand from 1972 to 1975. They detail our range of experiences as we dealt with a completely different culture and language.

We flew home to the U. S. in 1975 at the same time the Vietnam war ended. It did not personally touch us, although we could hear guns booming at night from a Thai air base outside of town.

One time in Bangkok, we made the acquaintance of a soldier taking R&R. To our amazement, he confessed in a tired voice, "All of the men in my unit chew betel nut leaves before we go into battle!" And when we were leaving that city, we noticed groups of refugees from Vietnam.

You could say I had a love-hate relationship with Thailand. People there were extremely nationalistic, so we could never feel at home and belong. I always felt at odds with the culture, which proved so different from mine.

I despaired at the poverty, the huge gap between the rich and the poor, and the relationships between men and women. I missed American conveniences like telephones and autos. We wilted in the heat. Yet I still left with many positive memories. We made several good friends. My heart warmed with the kindness shown to our children. I developed a real fondness for Thai food. Precepts from Buddhist philosophy inspired and helped me.

When I started teaching a few years after arriving back in the United States, I wrote a detailed paragraph on my resume that insured I'd always obtain a job. Not many Americans could say they learned enough of the native language to teach at a school for blind children. As part of my job, I also wrote my curriculum and raised money from friends in the community to fund it.

Even though it has been over 40 years and my children are middle-aged, those Thai experiences are fresh in my mind. I will never forget them.

Chapter 1
First Impressions

The bellhop unlocked the hotel room door and stood aside to allow us to enter. My husband, Joe, our two small sons, and I walked in, followed by our Peace Corps director, John. We surveyed the room. Suddenly, the boys both pointed to the walls and shouted, "Mommy! Daddy! What's moving there?"

What's moving indeed? Looking closely, we could see tiny lizards skittering around on the upper parts of the walls! Grabbing the boys, I turned around and started to walk out. "Sorry, John, but I can't stay in a room where critters might crawl on us!"

The bellhop stuttered, "Ma'am! Sir! Okay, okay!"

John added in a condescending tone, "Really, Pat, there's nothing to be afraid of. Those are *Chink-choes*, which we call geckos. You'll probably not find a room in this country without them! They won't jump on anyone. All they do is slither around on the walls and eat insects. Not bad companions at all!"

Now I blushed, a little embarrassed to have jumped to conclusions. "Well, okay," I replied, "but this country certainly is a strange place."

Our sons, Nate and Mattie, started yawning, and I felt pretty tired, too. John smiled. "I'll leave you here to get some rest and something to eat. About nine tomorrow morning we'll go for a tour."

As he walked out, he turned. "By the way, welcome to Bangkok!"

Our journey had started about ten days earlier. The four of us flew from my home state of Iowa to Seattle, where we stayed and visited my brother, sisters, and their families.

Then on to Hawaii, where we rested for a couple of days. Our sons became thrilled with the surf. They would run laughing into the breakers and then let us haul them out. We played that game over and over. Talk about an upper body workout for the parents!

Boarding Thai Airlines, we traveled to Bangkok. When we arrived in the early afternoon, John guided us through customs and drove us to the hotel. We didn't know what to expect when we entered those doors. Shocked, we saw a luxury establishment, one that would rival many in the States! The lobby boasted comfortable furniture with palm plants swaying a bit in glazed ceramic pots. Constructed of highly polished teak, the check-in desk proved imposing.

Our illusion that we were back home vanished with the *Chink-choes*, however! No matter what John said, did we dare close our eyes? Two large beds stood in the room. I put the boys to sleep in one, and then Joe and I laid down on the other. I determined to stay on guard, keeping awake to make sure those little critters didn't attack us! In only a few minutes, however, we all fell asleep, opening our eyes only at dinnertime.

The next morning we received a pleasant surprise. Breakfasting in the dining room of the hotel on typical Western fare of eggs, bacon, and fried potatoes, our eyes widened in amazement when the waiter set down the papaya we had ordered. The slices had to be 15 inches long!

We cut off little pieces for the boys. Then, spooning into it, we all agreed that it had to be the sweetest, most delicious fruit we had ever tasted. What a treat!

John picked us up at 9:00 a.m. as agreed. First, we stopped at the Peace Corps office to meet the staff and sign more paperwork. Then John drove us out of Bangkok. Used to the orderliness of traffic at home, we were stunned by the mess of all kinds of vehicles vying for space on the road.

Joe burst out, "This is crazy! How do people get anywhere? No traffic lights; just an occasional policeman directing at an intersection!" I nodded in agreement.

"Here's the secret to driving in Bangkok," John laughed. "Just look ahead. Don't ever look back or to the side."

"I'm feeling really bad culture shock right now!" I moaned. The fellows chuckled, but I actually meant every word.

Fortunately, our guide had a remedy for our disorientation. Leaving the city behind, we passed by rice fields, where peasants worked harvesting the grain. These peaceful scenes gave way to a small lake with a pagoda-style restaurant perched in the middle. Made of bamboo with a typical Thai roof, thatched with huge, dried banana leaves, it looked cool and welcoming. Walking on a bridge of bamboo with sturdy handrails brought us safely to the front door.

John ordered a buffet of Thai dishes. Soon, we feasted on a couple of types of curry, only mildly spiced, along with pork satay. These were flat pieces of meat marinated with peanut sauce, threaded on sticks, and grilled. Rice noodles cooked with eggs, bamboo shoots, bean sprouts, and bits of chicken tempted us. A bowl of fruit was set on the table, along with a container of rice. We drank cold, sweetened Thai tea. For dessert, one of the most scrumptious I have ever eaten: mangoes with sticky rice. This particular sweet is prepared by slicing the fruit thin, putting a couple of spoonfuls of sticky rice on the side, and covering the whole thing with a thin syrup made of sweetened coconut cream.

All during our time together, John told us basic cultural facts that we would be expected to learn. "Now, Pat and Joe," he instructed, "first of all, Thais regard the head as sacred. You know how you might pat a cute child on the head at home? Well, never, ever touch any Thai on the head. This is grossly insulting."

He went on, "On the other hand, it's also easy to offend with feet! You know how you might sit down and put your feet up at home? Well, never point the soles of your feet at a Thai person! As long as we're talking about insulting, you know how you beckon someone to come closer? Doing this with the palm up is the way Thais summon animals. Beckon people with the palm down. And Pat? Don't touch a monk, even by accident. This will land you in big trouble."

Promising more instruction later, John dropped us off at the hotel. Heads swimming with information, we collapsed on our beds for richly deserved naps.

Chapter 1
First Impressions

We had a free day before it became time for us to travel to our new home in Chiang Mai and chose to spend it strolling around Bangkok. The sewer smell swirled unpleasantly around us; the streets were dirty. Shops crowded one another, and little rickety food stands dotted the sidewalks. Thai people and a scattering of Chinese and Indians all jostled for space on the walkways. A few Westerners appeared here and there. The motorized vehicles in the streets belched fumes and the drivers honked for space. Can you imagine that we felt simply overcome with scenes so different from those at home?

The most heart-wrenching sight was the beggars who squatted in front of some stores. Dressed in rags, blind, or missing limbs, they called out to passersby and rattled their change boxes.

Mattie and Nate looked stunned. Questions flowed from them. "Why doesn't that man have any legs, Mommy? Why can't that man see?" We answered as best we could. After all, how do you explain such extreme hardship in the Third World to American children? Giving them coins to drop in a few of the boxes, we moved on.

On the sidewalk in front of a clothing store, an Indian man, dressed in a long gown with a turban on his head, gestured for us to come closer. He held a flute in his hands. A large wicker basket sat on the ground in front of him.

We moved closer. The man nodded, smiled at us, and started to play a mournful tune on his instrument. A helper, whom we had not noticed, quickly took the cover off the basket. A large cobra slowly unwound its coils, raised up, and swayed to the music. Joe grabbed me, I grabbed the boys, and we all stepped back. An audience had gathered, and a low chuckle ran through the crowd!

Turning to each other, we laughed weakly and shook our heads. "Tricia," Joe remarked, "doesn't it seem like we've traveled to the moon?"

One thing we realized right away. In appearance, we did not fit in! Our complexions and hair were light, our features Caucasian, but most of all, we were big!

At five-foot five and a half, I was considered medium height at home. But here I stood a head taller than many of the natives we passed on the street. And Joe! At six-foot two and 200 pounds, he was simply a giant. When our sons became tired of walking, he would hoist one up on his shoulders, and carry the other in his arms. That added another foot and a half in height!

As we swam in a sea of Asian languages, I remarked, "I have never felt sorrier for my Swedish immigrant grandparents. How awful it is not to understand a word that people are speaking!"

"I think the same thing about my Bohemian grandparents, who came to the States when my father was a baby," replied Joe.

Lost in commiseration, we stopped by a stand selling pork satays like we had eaten with John. "Now, what are the rules about food?" Joe mused. "We certainly don't want to get sick!"

"Cooked food is okay, and don't those satays smell good?" Nate and Mattie began moaning how hungry they felt, so we bought a few.

The stand next to it sold fried bananas. "They're cooked!" we chorused as we proceeded to devour them. Like the papaya, the bananas tasted sweeter and fresher than any we had ever eaten.

Dinner that night in the hotel proved an American's dream. We splurged and ate grilled steak, baked potatoes with butter and sour cream, salad, steamed asparagus, and for dessert, apple pie. As we chowed down, we didn't realize this was the last American food we would eat for almost a year.

"Chiang Mai sounds pretty good," Joe remarked. "Didn't John tell us that it is a small city nestled in the northern mountains? That foreigners love it, and the weather is a little better, not so hot in the winter months?"

"That's right," I replied. "He told us that it is much cleaner than Bangkok. Also, quite a few Western families live there, so we won't feel isolated."

With an early start, the next day we'd arrive in Chiang Mai. Joe and I decided that we could hardly wait!

Chapter 2

American Housekeeping, Thai Style

"Boon, Boon!" When I needed my Thai cook, she could never be found. After fruitlessly calling, I'd get up and walk through the dining room and kitchen.

Where could she be? Her little house stood just a couple of yards away. Our windows didn't have glass panes, and during the day, the wooden shutters stood wide open.

I knew Boon could hear me, so I would call some more. "Boon, Boon, *u-ti-nigh?*" (Where are you?) When Boon still refused to respond, I'd walk to her home, becoming increasingly irritated, for this happened every day.

When I stood a couple of feet from her front door, Boon would slowly emerge, surveying me with bright, black eyes. Her wiry, dark, shoulder-length hair was askew, and an insolent half-smile played on her lips.

Dressed in a Thai-American mixture, she appeared in an ankle-length, wrap-around black skirt with colored stripes at the bottom. Plastic thongs graced her feet. Her rose-colored blouse, a simple Western style, buttoned up the front.

As she sauntered closer, she'd fan herself with one hand and remove the dangling cigarette in her mouth with the other. Then, and only then, would Boon inquire, "*Ow-arai*," which, loosely translated, means, "What do you want?"

My husband and I had come to Thailand with our three-year-old twin sons as part of the Peace Corps in 1972. He loved to travel, I did not! However, jobs weren't easy to find for newly minted zoology professors. Against my better judgment, we ventured overseas.

After our arrival in Chiang Mai, John registered us at a local hotel. The next day he took us house-hunting. The two-story, teak wood home we selected proved one of a compound of three, all owned by a widow, Mrs. Panepa. A high cement wall surrounded them, and each house had a generous yard. Best of all, from my point of view, the kitchen boasted a gas stove and a refrigerator. The upstairs bathroom came equipped with a flush toilet and a shower. To my great delight, we had hot water, courtesy of a gas-powered water heater donated by our landlady.

Boon, Mrs. Panepa's helper, showed us around the house and negotiated for the rent with John. Her home stood in the middle of the compound. She and her husband, Maa, guarded against burglars and other intruders.

Maa also gardened, and Boon cleaned house and washed clothes for any tenants who occupied that house. In short, we were told, rent the house and we also hired a maid and a gardener.

"Why did we need servants? I asked.

"Everything is done by hand," John replied, "because there're very few washing machines, power lawn mowers, or other appliances. And shopping alone takes hours because supermarkets don't exist! You shop for food every day and bargain for the prices. You'll both be taking Thai language lessons and teaching. You won't have time to do all that work and spend time with your children."

"By the way," he added, "you'll need a cook too. Hmmm, maybe Boon can cook. It'd save money if you only needed one maid."

Unfortunately, I didn't understand the following conversation in Thai. If I had, I would've objected strenuously! Boon replied, "*Nit-noy,*" to every question. Too late, after we employed her, John told me that *nit-noy* meant "a little bit."

"You mean," I questioned him unbelievingly, "you just hired a cook for us who can only cook a little bit?"

"Right. But *may-pen-lie* (never mind), things will work out all right." John was a bachelor and obviously not in touch with the problems of feeding my family, a husband and two children who required three meals a day!

A month later, we hired another maid, Pun, to do the housecleaning, washing, and ironing, because Boon worked 12 hours a day trying to do everything. Now she could concentrate on cooking; a good thing!

So far, her meals had kept our stomachs roiling! Breakfast consisted of whole fried fish or scrambled eggs over rice, favorite Thai morning fare. Lunch and dinner proved alike: indistinguishable vegetables and bits of meat chopped at random and stir-fried, producing a colorless, lumpy mass. A pot of rice sat at the table.

Boon was puzzled that we ate the stuff! After all, we were Americans. What about the military PX cans she always opened and heated for the other tenants? With the help of our other Thai neighbor, Murrie, who spoke excellent English, I tried convincing her we didn't have PX privileges. She found this very hard to grasp because other renters had always purchased food there!

While Joe and I suffered Boon's meals, too exhausted by work, culture shock, and heat to eat much anyway, our children reacted quite differently. They staged a hunger strike, eating only milk from the local German dairy and fruit.

Boon was a mother, too. She proved almost as distressed as I was when day followed day and the boys became perceptibly thinner. To help remedy the situation, she bought tiny quails' eggs at the market. The children greedily ate these as soon as Boon cooked them. Her husband then climbed a tree and brought down even tinier birds' eggs which the kids loved.

But Nate and Mattie still moaned and complained, particularly at breakfast: "Rice, ye-e-echt! For breakfast? Why can't we have eggs and toast, oatmeal, or pancakes? And why can't you cook it, Mommy? We don't like that awful woman in the kitchen. We can't even understand what she says!"

I gave up on the idea that the kids would get used to a Thai-style breakfast. Anyway, fish and rice in the early morning created lumps in my stomach, too. Since my language lessons didn't start until 8:00 a.m., I told Boon to come a little later, and I would make breakfast for my family.

With difficulty, I located wheat flour and yeast in the market, and I used my spare time in the afternoon to bake bread.

Chapter 2
American Housekeeping, Thai Style

With the high heat and humidity, the loaves rose quickly and tasted heavenly! I also found some tinned imported oatmeal at an outrageous price, but the boys welcomed it like an old friend. By further sleuthing, I uncovered small containers of plain yogurt in a shop that carried Western food. I used one as a starter for my old yogurt recipe. The boys stopped moaning in the morning, and my stomach stopped doing flip-flops.

Breakfast was solved, but at the price of increasing my work load and decreasing my cook's. Would lunch and dinner fare the same? Fortunately not. Boon learned to fix delicious Thai soups like *kwuit-deo-nam* with meatballs, noodles, lettuce, and bean sprouts, and another, *Khow-tom*, which was rice with chopped pork, dried shrimp, and greens. We all loved those hot soups, so those became our basic luncheon menu.

Boon also searched for other Thai dishes to add variety. She wowed us with dried red beef and sticky rice. However, I surprised her with my reaction when she beamingly served stewed chicken intestines, cut up in half-inch long pieces.

"There's no way I can eat this, Boon!" I insisted emphatically.

"But, Mrs. Pat," she wheedled, "these are a favorite of Thai women." After stout denials on my part, she never prepared that dish again!

With breakfast and lunch out of the way, I longed for Western food. *Perhaps I can teach Boon to make hamburgers*, I thought.

Communication proved the main obstacle. For marketing and ordinary household tasks, I consulted a list of words my tutor had written both phonetically and in Thai. When

Boon could not understand my pronunciation, she read the printed word. If even this failed, Murrie translated. Of course, from necessity, my vocabulary rapidly increased. After a year, my Thai and Boon's English had both improved to the extent that we communicated in a weird mixture of the two, which she dubbed, *Phazar Pat* (Pat's language).

But back in the beginning, teaching Boon to cook proved a long, drawn-out, arduous task. Trying to bridge the language gap, I worked with her each step of the way making hamburgers. We chopped up beef from the market and bought expensive hamburger buns from the store. Then I showed her how to shape and fry the patties, and put the sandwiches together with ketchup, mustard, sliced onions, and tomatoes.

After three times making them together, I thought Boon was ready for a solo flight. Putting my best Thai forward, I announced, "Boon, now you know how to make hamburgers. Tomorrow, when the boys and I come home for lunch, we'll have delicious hot hamburgers cooked by you—right?"

Unfortunately, wrong! We struggled with hamburgers several times before I gave up and went back to Thai fare. The hamburgers either came burned to a crisp or so raw we couldn't eat them. And always, always as cold as could be. In fact, except for soups, I could never get Boon to serve us hot food. After she ignored many requests, a friend told me that Thais don't consider hot food necessary. If they want a food "hot" they put peppers in it—and believe me, it burns all the way down!

Surprisingly, Boon's failure with hamburgers did not bother her. In fact, she generally proved less inclined to follow instructions. With Pun doing the housecleaning and washing, Boon only marketed, ran errands, and fixed two meals a day. Her work day had been cut to about six hours for the same salary.

My frustration pushed higher and higher, and one day Boon hit my limits. That particular afternoon, I was baking cakes for the boys' birthday party. It proved quite a time-consuming job, since I needed three cakes and could only bake one layer at a time in my small oven. Since Boon didn't know how to bake, I assigned her dishwashing. After a while, she complained, "I'm getting so tired washing all these pots and pans—why don't you do it?"

That's it! I huffed. So angry I could barely finish the cakes, I fumed to myself, *Now my cook wants me to be her maid!*

That evening, I announced to my husband that Boon and I were through. "I have too much work to do," I exploded, "to put up with that lazy, useless woman any longer. She's had enough chances. She has to go now!"

But Joe, while just as exasperated as me, replied, "How can we fire her when we live next door? You know, in this country when a servant goes with the house, you don't fire him, you move!"

Joe's coworkers, who explained Thai culture quite helpfully, also told him that Thais don't fire an incompetent person from a job. First of all, they select employees very carefully. If the person hired still proves inadequate, though, they just live with his faults and share his undone work. It's also an unforgivable sin to demote a person from a higher-status job to a lower one.

Our options appear limited, I mused, *because I don't want to move!* I also shuddered at the thought of Boon's revenge if we demoted her to maid. Cursing John for getting us into this position, my husband and I pondered a solution.

We finally decided to threaten Boon with dismissal anyway, to see what would happen. Since women have all the power in family and business life in Thailand, I alone approached Boon. As I did so, I felt like a mother locked in battle with a moody teenaged daughter!

"Boon, you're a cook now," I began. "It's a very important job. It means that you have to cook the foods we want and prepare it to our taste. For instance, I want you to serve hot meals, prepare Western food, and bake bread. I can teach you all of this, and then you'll really be a cook. Otherwise, we'll have to hire someone else, for I'm getting tired of doing my job and yours too."

My speech released a torrent of words and feeling from ordinarily sullen Boon, as she exploded in very untypical Thai fashion.

"You want me to be a good cook," she replied heatedly, "but how can you expect that when you don't pay me a cook's wages? My friend also works for Westerners and she makes twice as much money as I do. Her employers eat only dinner at home, and she has a servant to do the dishes!"

Now I realized that status with her friend was involved. Boon wanted to be a "real" cook with a salary to prove it. Unfortunately for us, however, she didn't know that a good cook earned her wages by her competence.

Chapter 2
American Housekeeping, Thai Style

Boon sullenly served another lousy meal that night, and my husband easily guessed that my speech hadn't impressed her. At that point, I realized the relationship between Boon and me must change.

As I explained to my husband, "I've been treating Boon in a friendly fashion, like my mother managed her Italian cleaning lady. I've been expecting her to do the jobs I ask her to do. Mother never had a problem with Mrs. Fietta, who always did excellent work, easily meeting Mother's expectations.

"In fact, Mrs. Fietta almost became a member of the family. She and Mother took coffee breaks together; sometimes she stayed for dinner. I remember the time she showed my sister and me how to make pizza. Our family liked her so much I invited her to my wedding!"

I went on, "But your Thai coworkers have told us that treating Boon like an equal won't work. To her, that just means she doesn't need to work hard, or follow instructions. A friend, unlike a master, forgives work undone."

"Remember how horrified we felt when Boon first served us drinks?" I asked Joe. "How she shuffled in on her knees? I don't want to put her back on her knees, but I'm going to treat her more like a child. Check up on her frequently, question her activities around the house, and especially monitor her outlay of money in the market much more closely than I have been doing."

Joe agreed. "There's something else we can do," he reasoned. "The teachers at school tell me that when there is difficulty, Thais seek to settle it through a third party. It might be better if we could find someone else to talk to Boon, someone she looks up to and respects."

Reflecting on this, we arrived at yet another plan to motivate reluctant Boon. We'd enlist our landlady to our side. Seated in Mrs. Panepa's elegant home, I spoke to her in my fractured Thai, since she knew no English whatsoever. Frustrated with Boon and worried about accurate communication, I struggled with the unfamiliar language. Eventually, I succeeded, because Mrs. Panepa proved an extremely polite and patient lady. As I related my battle with Boon, Mrs. Panepa's eyes widened slightly, although she still smiled. Assuring me she'd speak with Boon immediately, she bid me a pleasant goodnight.

I doubted Mrs. Panepa's effectiveness, though. *How could such a gentle woman,* I thought, *impress our cook, who seemed a bit of a ruffian?*

But the next day found Boon terribly agitated! "Why did you talk to Mrs. Panepa?" she demanded. "I've always told you to speak to me first about any problem. Then, if necessary, I'd talk to her!"

"But Boon!" I exclaimed. "This time the problem is you! I felt I had no other choice!"

"Okay, okay," she replied reluctantly. "What do you want me to do?"

I could hardly believe my ears! "Let's bake bread first," I suggested. "That'll help me greatly, since we eat about a loaf a day. If you can make good bread, people will realize you're a successful cook."

Although I tried to sound confident, I thought, *Pat, you're crazy. Here's a gal who can't even fry hamburgers, and you want her baking bread!*

However, Boon surprised me greatly by learning the first time. Bread rose very quickly in the tropical heat, but also, Boon confided, "It's so easy to knead the bread because we wash our clothes this way!"

True enough. Clothes were scrubbed in big tubs with sort of a kneading motion, and Thai women developed terrifically strong, muscled hands.

Boon's skill rapidly improved until she could bake delicious, high loaves. The Thai neighbors admired her and even Mrs. Panepa, a skilled cook, sought Boon for bread-making lessons. Boon beamed with her success and eagerly inquired, "What's next?"

Banana bread followed, because of the abundance of Thai bananas. A tree even grew in our backyard! Then I taught Boon to make beef stew, American salad, and salad dressing. "But cooking lessons drag on forever," I complained to some friends one afternoon, "since Boon speaks so little English and can't read my recipes either. At this rate, we'll have left Thailand before she can fix more than one good meal!"

Sarah came to my rescue with the perfect solution. "My cook is absolutely fabulous," she asserted. "She can cook American, French, and Chinese, as well as Thai food. Everything she cooks is delectable. In fact, she's so good that right now she would like to give lessons. Would you be interested?"

I thanked Sarah profusely. The perfect answer to our problems!

Boon took a taxi over to Sarah's house, and soon we hungrily devoured many new dishes. For example, we savored chicken baked in coconut cream and soy sauce, marinated pork shish-kabob, Chinese egg rolls, and Oriental sweet and sour fish with vegetables.

Wow! Did we eat well for a change! Boon also learned to prepare the delicious, spicy Thai curries to our tender tastes.

Wonder of wonders, cooked food also appeared on the table hot! In fact, if we lagged a bit getting to the table, Boon chided, "Come and eat. Your dinner's getting cold!"

Boon even scolded Joe when he occasionally stopped for a drink on the way home and arrived late. "Where have you been?" she would admonish. "Out drinking with your worthless friends, I'll bet, and now your dinner is cold!"

Joe would moan that it was bad enough having his wife nag him, let alone his cook. Boon would wink and smile at me as if to say, *Just let me handle him and he won't get out of line very often!*

Boon learned more than cooking at Sarah's house, however. She became more responsible for her position as cook and manager of our household, following instructions better and being more helpful about running errands. She also complained much less about her duties and salary. She had observed Sarah's cook's much greater workload, which included afternoon babysitting and cooking for evening parties several nights a week.

Irascible Boon never adopted an air of complete servitude, however. She'd never come when I called and remained quick to express an opinion or push her interests.

But I grew to admire her. No wonder she always pushed for salary increases. Boon's paycheck supported her aged father and her sister's family, as well as her own. Eager for her children to receive good educations, she paid tuition to private schools. At that time, free public schools only went to third grade.

Finally, we had only a few months before we left Thailand. I could hardly wait! One day Boon and I stood chatting about the coming move and she remarked, "Your friend Sarah's family is leaving soon too, Mrs. Pat. They are taking their cook with them!"

"Well, that doesn't surprise me, Boon. You know, her husband is a medical doctor and the head of a children's hospital here. He makes a lot of money! I suppose Sarah would like to entertain in the States like she does here."

Suddenly, Boon pleaded, "Mrs. Pat. I want to go to America. Take me with you!"

Flabbergasted, I paused a moment before answering. True, Boon and I had gone through a lot together, and wow, what a super cook she had become! But—there was no way—just no way. "I'm sorry, Boon, we can't. We don't have the money Sarah's husband earns. Joe doesn't even have a job and we have to find a place to live!"

Boon looked skeptical. I could practically see her thinking, *Aren't all Americans rich?*

Over the next week or two, she teasingly mentioned the possibility of her traveling with us a few times, but finally accepted that it couldn't be done.

The time came for us to leave. We had crated our furniture, packed our bags, and stood ready to jump in the Peace Corps director's car. Only then did Boon and I bid goodbye. We spoke only a few words, but gazed for a few long moments into each other's eyes.

What a character! I'll never forget her.

Sometimes, back in the States, I would mention our experience in Thailand. A woman friend might sigh and breathe, "What I wouldn't give for three servants: a cook, a maid, and a gardener. What a life you must have led!"

Rolling my eyes and chuckling a bit, I'd say, "You don't know the half of it!"

Chapter 3
Culture Conundrums

"*See dum*," my Chiang Mai landlady Mrs. Panepa remarked, gracefully pointing to me. I felt absolutely flummoxed. What in blazes did that mean?

"*See dum*," she repeated, this time stroking her cheek. We had lived in Thailand a few months and had taken language lessons, but I still drew a complete blank. I glanced helplessly at our other neighbor, Murrie, a tiny, vivacious Thai lady who spoke excellent English.

"Pat," she answered quickly, "*see* means color and *dum* is brown. Mrs. Panepa is trying to say that you have tanned from the sun."

"Ohhh. Thank you, Murrie." I turned to Mrs. Panepa, stroked my own cheek, and murmured, "*See dum*." She beamed.

How frustrating, I thought. *We took Thai lessons for two months, and then I took instruction part-time while teaching at the blind school. No one ever thought to teach me color words, one of the first things we teach toddlers at home!*

Thai people did seem to be pleased at our poor attempts at their language. I remember the first word I learned: *dee* (good). When Joe and I biked to the market, I tried out my new word. Every time I said "*dee*," the person would smile and say, "*Phoot Thai dee muck.*" (You speak Thai very well.) I felt delighted; however, I certainly had a long ways to go.

Of course, learning Thai is like learning a song. You need to know not only the words but the tune as well, since Thai is a tonal language. The frustrating thing is that the same word can mean different things, depending on its tone. I found it hard to remember which note went with which word. At least I could produce the tones, since I had grown up singing and playing instruments. My poor husband, though, could not carry a tune. His Thai sounded like a bunch of flatware clanging together.

The Peace Corps had assigned me to the School for the Blind, a children's institution. That made sense since I was a certified teacher. But how do you teach blind people when you don't know the language and they can't see your gestures?

Until I had more words under my belt, my tutor would come to the school on Mondays, Wednesdays, and Fridays. I would use that opportunity to learn school words. Then I taught Tuesdays and Thursdays. As I became more proficient, my lessons were two days a week, and I taught three. Finally, the lessons quit altogether.

Fortunately, there were two young women teachers, Pranee and Sumalee, as well as the headmistress, who all spoke excellent English. I could refer to any of them for help.

Family Life

Family life proved much different in Thailand than at home. In the States, most of the women I knew who had children weren't gainfully employed. However, in Thailand, often both mother and father worked, and the grandparents or other extended family might care for the small children. Preschools also proved widely available, although costly. If the family owned a shop or restaurant, the children might be taken to work.

Small children were overly indulged as far as I was concerned. A grandmother might chase after a small child with a bowl of rice. This astounded me. My boys sat at the table with us in special seats after they turned about a year and a half.

Role of Women in Thailand

In fact, the role of women in Thailand puzzled us. We assumed that Thai women would be subservient to men. However, in the market, we noticed that only women tended the cash registers. Going to the bank one day, we felt quite startled to see that the six tellers in front all were young men. A woman sat behind them at a large desk. The teller drawers were empty. Instead, they handed deposits to the lady, and, in turn, she gave withdrawal money back to them for the customers. It all flowed very smoothly, but she proved definitely in charge.

When we stopped at the hardware store for something Joe wanted, the clerk addressed me. That surprised me, because I knew nothing about hardware. Why didn't she question my husband?

One day we went to our woman dentist's office to pay our bill. A young man answered and informed us that the dentist was gone.

"We know how much the bill is," I told him. "Can we just give the money to you?"

"Oh, no," he replied laughing. "Come back when she's here. I would just spend it!"

At Chiang Mai University, where Joe worked, many women taught. In fact, the head of his department was a woman. The fairer sex also served in the country's legislature. However, at home, in the early '70s, teaching and nursing were the most common professional career paths for U.S. women. The glass ceiling stayed firmly in place.

Why did Thai women seem so much more liberated professionally than American women?

By now our heads spun. Just what was the role of women in this country, we asked each other. John, our Peace Corp director, gave us some helpful information.

He informed us, "Most marriages in Thailand are still arranged. Husbands and wives don't usually have the strong emotional ties that we Americans expect. Men are very attached to their mothers and women to their children."

John went on, "Young people don't date. A man and woman holding hands or kissing in public would be absolutely scandalous. However, men can hold hands with each other and women can do the same. Wives control the purse strings in their families. A man might often go out with other men in the evenings. But his wife gives him an allowance so she knows exactly how much fun he can have! Here women are the responsible ones; men are considered butterflies."

However, a dark side emerged in Thai marital arrangements. In their society at that time, it seemed quite permissible for a man to have more than one wife, or mistress, as long as he could support them. Prostitution was prevalent.

Married men, single men, it didn't matter; any man could indulge and many did. Northern Thai women proved much in demand for the oldest profession because of their beauty. In fact, very poor rural families might even sell a daughter into prostitution in order to survive.

Customs and Religion

On the other hand, many customs proved benign and actually quite interesting. You know the ubiquitous American greeting, "Hi, how are you?" In Thailand, the common greeting is, "*By nigh?*" (Where are you going?) One answers in kind: "*By bon,*" (I'm going home) or any other place one happens to be heading. We fell easily into that practice. It seemed to satisfy curiosity and give the impression that we knew more words than we did!

There were also beliefs that I found deeply moving and even instructive. The majority of Thais were very devout Buddhists. Unlike some "Sunday Christians" that I grew up with—people who devoutly prayed, sang, and listened to the sermon in church, and then lied and cheated the rest of the week—Thais practiced their religion every day. Almost every man spent some time in a monastery during his lifetime, and women might serve as Buddhist nuns.

Their religion believed in reincarnation. Thai Buddhists maintained that a person must be happy and contented in this life. If he could do that, in the next one he would be placed higher. However, woe if he couldn't. Because then he might come back as a dog, the very lowest form of life in Thailand!

This contentment radiated throughout Thailand. When we entered markets, stores, and restaurants, the only sounds would be the soft music of their language flowing around us.

And how about the American legend of the "self-made" man—someone who starts out very poor and fights his way upward in life by his own determination, wits, and talent? This belief seemed absent in Thailand. Group process to solve problems was encouraged. I personally came to think that a combination of these ideas would be better than either alone.

In truth, I loved some tenants of Buddhist philosophy. In my struggle with a culture vastly different from mine, I found these helpful. For instance, I liked the saying that, as far as emotion is concerned, life is best lived following the "middle path." I also absorbed the idea that life is like a wheel. If the wheel is up and you're happy, that's great, but don't relish it too much! Because life being what it is, the wheel will eventually turn, and you might be miserable. On the other hand, if you are unhappy, don't wallow in this feeling. Eventually, the wheel will turn again, and you'll be happy and content once more.

As appointed representatives of the United States government, we needed to tread "the middle path" and try not to offend our hosts. Ugly Americans need not apply!

While there were aspects of Thai culture that made me despair, such as open prostitution and glaring poverty, still I learned to love the Thai people for the good manners, contentment, and happiness they showed most of the time. Their acceptance of their place in life often astonished and instructed me. I admired the strong, beautiful Thai women. And I still eagerly enjoy Thai food on a regular basis!

The chance to enter and live intimately in another culture is a chance many Americans never get. In those three years, I became alternately charmed, inspired, astonished, frustrated, joyful, and angry. Even though it was more than forty years ago, I will never forget my experiences or the lessons I learned there.

Chapter 4
The Blind Leading the Blind

The tuc-tuc (a pick-up truck with benches installed in the back for people to sit on) turned off the highway onto a narrow, dirt road. The vehicle swerved to miss some potholes and bounced in and out of others. Sitting in the back on a narrow bench, I clung to the side to avoid being thrown to the floor! The moist, tropical heat hugged me tight, making it difficult to breathe. I mopped my face with my handkerchief. As usual, the freshness from my morning shower had worn off in minutes.

We jolted to a stop before open gates protecting a wide cement driveway. Climbing out of the pick-up truck, I waved to the driver. "Bye-bye," I called. "*Cop-coon-cah.*" (Thank you.)

He grinned. "Bye-bye," he answered.

I shuddered, sighed deeply, and resolutely walked up the long driveway to the buildings in front of me. A two-story, white painted structure greeted me. The large windows were empty of glass. Instead, decorative metal strips filled the spaces, just like ours at home. These were called *quomoy* bars, a common barrier against thieves. Wooden shutters at each side provided additional protection. The roof flowed over the patio, joining the main building to a couple of smaller ones.

This was my first day at my Peace Corps job teaching English to blind students, and I felt quite apprehensive. Although an experienced teacher, I still had many questions. My main fear concerned teaching the children when I couldn't speak Thai very well yet, and they couldn't even see my gestures.

As usual, John, the Peace Corps director, had answered offhandedly, "*May-pen-lai.*" (Never mind.) "You'll manage." I'd visited the week before and met the headmistress, Ajahn Karawek. Short and stout, with black, permed hair, she'd glared at me from behind her tinted glasses, barely noticing my presence. Today she stood on the patio with students and teachers lined up in front of her. I closed the gap between us quickly and pressed my palms together in front of my chest. As I bowed deeply to acknowledge her as my boss, I greeted her, So-wat-dee-cah." (General greeting from a woman, meaning hello or goodbye.)

With the same sour look on her face, she barely bent her head and returned my greeting: "*So-wat-dee-cah.*"

"Will you please translate my English if the children don't understand me?" I requested. She nodded. I counted only 20 children, which surprised me. Two Thai teachers, also blind, stood at one side of the group.

The students ranged in age from a tiny girl about seven or eight to a strapping lad who might have been eighteen. Dressed in the typical Thai student school uniform, the girls wore white blouses and blue skirts, with their hair cut chin-length with bangs. The boys sported white shirts, blue shorts, and crew cuts. Some of the children stood awkwardly, with their heads tilted to one side and their chins raised.

Smiling, I spoke, "Hello! I am Mrs. Pat, your new teacher."

Without any prompting, they answered, "Hello, Mrs. Pat." They all grinned.

"Ah! You speak English so well." I commented. The children giggled, pleased with my compliment.

I gazed quickly at their faces and my stomach did flip-flops. While most had eyes simply closed, others were startling. For instance, one boy's eyes actually popped out from their sockets! As I looked at the Thai teachers, I noticed the older, shorter one's face, neck, and arms were lightly pocked with scars. Her eyes stared blankly at me. The iris and pupil in each eye were gone. Only the whites faced the world.

Whew! Nausea threatened to overcome me, but I continued to smile and speak warmly. Of course, years of teaching experience helped me keep my equilibrium. Softly, I asked each child's name and each answered, "My name is _____, Mrs. Pat."

When I came to the teachers, the older one with the empty eyes grasped my hands firmly. "Mrs. Pat, we're so glad you're here. Welcome! My name is Pranee." She spoke perfect English, with only a trace of a musical Thai accent.

I laughed, delighted at her enthusiasm! "Thank you, Pranee. I'm sure we'll enjoy working together."

Sneaking a side glance at the headmistress, I noticed that her expression had softened. Suddenly, I understood. Very protective of her charges, she didn't know how I would react to each one's appearance.

From behind the children, my tutor appeared. "Mrs. Pat," she called. "It's time for your lesson."

"Yes, I'm coming, Ajahn Buppha. Children, today I will have a Thai lesson and tomorrow we will have an English lesson. *So-wat-dee-cah*! Bye-bye!"

Inside our classroom, we sat facing each other. I remarked, "The children are so cheerful, smiling and laughing even though they're—"

At this point, my teacher interrupted me. She had been hired to teach us not only the Thai language, but also to understand and respect the culture. Softly, but with snapping eyes, she replied, "You mean you're surprised blind children can be happy?"

Shamefacedly, I nodded.

"You know," she continued, "curious about them myself, I asked the headmistress to tell me about their homes and families. Apparently, most of these children come from small, country villages. The Thai government sends agents to find them so they can be helped. The headmistress told me the children are often found tied up. This isn't because the parents are cruel, but the villages aren't safe for them. The families usually live in bamboo homes that are built on stilts. Blind people could fall down the homes' ladders or wander into open fire pits in the villages.

I asked, "Does anyone know if blindness in Thai children is caused by anything in particular?"

"In fact, doctors have found that lack of vitamin A causes much of it."

Incredulous, I asked, "In spite of the luscious fruits in this country, like mangos and papayas?

Reproachfully, she muttered, "Not everyone can afford them, Mrs. Pat."

Tears filled my eyes while my cheeks burned with embarrassment. We Americans knew so little about the problems in the rest of the world. "Well," I ventured, "isn't it good the children can live here, Ajahn? Compared to their homes, I imagine this school must seem like a paradise. No wonder they're so joyful. But then, my husband and I have noticed everyone in Thailand acts happy!"

Now my instructor smiled gently. "It's our Buddhist faith that requires us to be contented in the life we've been given. We believe we'll have many lives. If we're satisfied with this one, then in the next, our status will improve. If we're discontented, however, we might come back as dogs!"

Yes, I mused, *things are so different here.* In Thailand, instead of pampered pooches like ours, dogs were wretched scavengers riddled with diseases like rabies.

"Thank you, Ajahn, I always appreciate it when you tell me about your culture. Many of us Americans could benefit by Thai philosophy."

Then I abruptly changed the subject. "Now, here are the words and phrases I'd like to learn for my English lesson. Tomorrow morning will arrive shortly!"

Once I started teaching, I fell in love with the children. Of course, it wasn't easy since they couldn't see my gestures. But what a delightful group! There were no discipline problems, the students listened carefully, and they always tried to obey. And what happy children! Being their teacher proved simply a joy. When I arrived at school on my motorcycle, all the students would run toward me, shouting, "Mrs. Pat! Mrs. Pat!" If I felt grumpy or stressed when I arrived, it simply disappeared under this deluge of enthusiasm!

After about three months, my language tutor and I parted company. I had learned barely enough "school Thai" to get along, but I could always count on Pranee to help me with the words I needed. Of course, I said enough "bloopers" to keep the school staff laughing. One of the funniest happened when the headmistress told me the children wanted to dance. "Everyone knows blind people simply can't do that!" she remarked smugly.

"You know," I replied, "we brought a small record player and a box of children's songs with us. If you'd like, I'll look through it and see what I can find."

The next day, I happily reported that two dances might work: the Hokey Pokey and the Bunny Hop. Ajahn Karawek gave her permission for me to go ahead.

On the appointed day, the kids gathered in the classroom with me. Outside the open windows stood most of the staff of the school, waiting patiently for blind children to dance!

We started with the Hokey Pokey. Since it was a circle dance, they learned quickly. The Bunny Hop came next. I placed the students in a line. Each one had his hands on the waist of the person in front. We learned each hop before we put it together. I started the music and, wonder of wonders, the line moved forward, with the kids hopping correctly.

I had placed a partially sighted child in front, who led the line well. Almost too well. Soon the group approached the door. I called out, "*Rao, rao.*" (Go fast.)

The leader kept going. "*Rao, rao,*" I called again.

The boy in front was almost out the door. Desperately, I tried to think. *Why wasn't he stopping?*

Then Pranee's voice sounded, just loud enough for me to hear. "Mrs. Pat, *Yut, yut!*"

Of course! I had mixed up *rao* and *yut*. *Rao* means go fast and *yut* means stop.

"*Yut, yut,*" I called. Magically, the line stopped quickly! Again, I was deeply grateful to Pranee. I really didn't mind the amusement of the staff, even at my expense!

As time went on, Pranee, another teacher named Sumalee, and I became friends. The latter looked quite pretty with her luxurious black hair, smooth complexion, and classic features. She usually dressed in a blouse and a flowing skirt belted at the waist. Partially sighted, her eyes weren't as afflicted as her companion's.

I felt sorry for Pranee. Thais prized feminine beauty, perhaps even more so than Westerners! With her pocked skin and white eyes, Pranee proved not even remotely attractive. But her obvious intelligence, charm, and absolute joy of living drew people to her.

Any time we had a break, Sumalee and Pranee would each grab one of my hands and steer me toward a couple of benches placed on the front lawn. There we chatted while continuing to hold hands.

Growing up in a homophobic time and place, at first I felt extremely uncomfortable with this behavior. My American women friends and I only expressed such emotion with our female relatives. *How could Thais be so different from us?* I wondered.

We learned that a young man and young woman couldn't show affection for each other in public. However, a pair of boys or two girls could hold hands in public with no repercussions.

I gradually became used to this custom. In fact, it seemed to make our conversations more personal. And since Pranee spoke English so well, I could talk easily with her.

One day, out of the blue, Pranee asked me, "Mrs. Pat, would you like to know how I became blind?"

"Yes, I would," I answered. "I've been curious about it, but didn't want to ask and risk embarrassing you."

"Don't worry about that! My blindness is just a fact of life and I'm used to it. Well, Mrs. Pat, I was born during World War II in Bangkok. The Japanese occupied Thailand then. Food and medicine became scarce. As a baby I caught smallpox. I don't know how I survived, but my skin became pocked all over and I lost my sight."

Tears dimmed my eyes. "I'm so sorry, Pranee."

"Mrs. Pat! Don't cry! Life is good for me. Fortunately, I attended the School for the Blind in Bangkok, which is where I learned to speak English so well. Now I have a good job, with people who're kind to me, as well as plenty to eat and clothes to wear. Many sighted people aren't as lucky as I am."

Quite true. In our travels around Thailand, we'd seen ragged, diseased beggars and plenty of people living in tumble-down shacks. Riding through the countryside, we'd witnessed men and women breaking rocks for a living, sweating in the searing, tropical sun. Once, in downtown Bangkok, we'd even witnessed the unbelievable sight of a dying woman. She lay sprawled beside a fountain, and passersby casually strolled around her with unseeing eyes.

"Joe!" I'd cried, walking toward her. "We've got to do something!"

He gently pulled me away, his voice reflecting great sadness. "No, no, Tricia. She might have a contagious disease. And, anyway, who would we call?"

I sighed and turned to go with him and the children. "Okay, I guess you're right."

As I continued working at the blind school, I enjoyed one definite advantage of teaching there. Ajahn Karawek allowed me to bring one of my children to school with me occasionally. Staff and students always greeted the boys enthusiastically. In general, Thais loved little children. Joe and I had often seen whole families working in their businesses together, with the youngest ones running around the restaurant or shop.

Once, when Nate rode with me to work, I took him over to meet Sumalee and Pranee. With the uncanny perception of the blind, Pranee called to me, "Who's with you, Mrs. Pat? A little person?"

"My son, Nathan," I replied proudly. "He's four years old."

Smiling, she held out her arms. "Ohh, come here, Nathan! Let me hug you!"

But he took one look at her, started screaming, and fled behind me, clutching my skirt!

I felt acutely embarrassed, forgetting for a moment how my own stomach had clenched when I'd first met Pranee. "Nathan, Nathan," I soothed. "Please come and meet Pranee. She's a very nice lady, and she loves little children!"

But he shook his head and buried it further in my skirts. Clasping her hand, I whispered, "I'm so sorry, Pranee. He doesn't mean to hurt your feelings."

But she actually laughed! "No, no, Mrs. Pat, it truly is okay. Many children are afraid when they see my face."

What a woman! I thought as I gave her arm consoling pats.

After two years, my service at the school ended, although we stayed in Thailand for one more year before going home. Of course, I'll never forget the people I met, especially those at the blind school, and most of all Pranee. As teachers often say, I learned more than I taught.

Two years later, in 1977, my circumstances had completely changed. I was a divorced, single mother looking for a job. As I sat with an elementary principal in his office, I watched as he began to read my one-page resume. He appeared a colorless man, with his hair, suit, and tie all gray. Even his complexion appeared washed in the same tone. But he smiled at me kindly.

Hmmm. What does he think of me? I mused.

As an answer, Mr. Leonard glanced up. His watery, blue eyes widened and his mouth was slightly agape. "My, my! You actually taught Thai blind children while learning their language?"

I nodded.

"Then you wrote your own curriculum and adapted lessons for them?"

"That's right."

"You also signed up American volunteers and raised money for your projects?"

"That too."

"Well, I must say, this is very impressive, Mrs. Lidrich."

Fervently, I replied, "Thank you, and believe me, it wasn't easy!"

Needless to say, I got the job teaching kindergarten students.

Chapter 5
Blind School Postscript

After concluding my story about the blind school in Chiang Mai, Thailand, I began wondering: Is the school still in existence? If so, what is it like? After all, only about twenty students attended when I taught there from 1972 to 1974. Of course, I immediately ventured onto the Internet. And what a surprise I found!

In the last 40 years, the school has grown to over 200 students, with 26 teachers and 39 other staff. As in the 1970s, the children are mostly from rural northern Thai villages. Their curriculum conforms to the Thai government's standards, also including Braille training in Thai and English. In addition, students learn to use white canes for independent travel. (I remember when the headmistress angrily rejected my request for this same skill to be taught!) The curriculum also provides computer skills, music, sports, foreign languages (English and French), and occupational training.

Pictures of the vocational program interested me. They showed students busy making baskets and weaving cloth. Everything made is on sale to raise funds for the school.

Massage is also taught, perhaps a logical occupation for blind students. What progress since my time with them!

Another program that truly fits the children's rural background is learning agricultural skills. I looked at several pictures showing the older boys and girls working in the rice fields, caring for farm animals from ducks to cattle, and raising vegetables and fruits. Kitchen skills are taught there also. This is held in a village about 15 miles from the school. It is a useful transition program, since many of these students will return to their homes in the countryside.

Before moving to the school, the children might have been restrained to keep them from harming themselves, like falling into an open fire pit. After learning kitchen and farming skills, as well as independent travel, they can return as useful members of their communities.

Another surprise for me was that the school received funding from the Mudita Trust, founded by one Thai woman, Surapee Mudita Karnasuta. Growing up in a well-off family, Mrs. Surapee became aware of prostitution at an early age. One day when her father was driving around Bangkok with her, she noticed several beggar children.

When she asked why they wore rags and asked people for money, her father replied, "They are the children of prostitutes, women who have to sell their bodies because they are very poor. Their offspring are not allowed to go to school and will probably follow their mothers into the same trade."

This horror story stuck with Mrs. Surapee. As an adult, she received an advanced degree in Australia and then moved to England. Seeing a newspaper story about child prostitution in Thailand, she remembered her early shock at learning of the probable fate of the young beggars.

She established the Mudita Trust in 1992, dedicated to the prevention of child prostitution in Thailand through education. According to Mrs. Surapee, there were ten schools that received funds from the Trust in 2013. The Chiang Mai School for the Blind was one. Fundraisers, charitable gifts, as well as 10% of the profits from her Thai restaurant, provide the money for these schools. Mrs. Surapee has received many awards for her good works.

The name Mudita means "rejoicing in others' good fortune." It was suggested by a Buddhist monk who happened to be Mrs. Surapee's spiritual advisor. He had also bestowed the same name on her a few years before because of her unselfish nature.

Of course, I was happy to learn of the expansion of the blind school and the funds that have been bestowed on it and other schools by the Mudita Trust.

As a result, the Chiang Mai School for the Blind is adequately funded and its students' lives are filled with hope for the future.

Chapter 6
Motorcycle Mama

In my dream, I perched on a motorcycle wearing leathers and a full face helmet. As I drove down the roads of Chiang Mai I scattered other vehicles in my wake. The warm air breezed by me. Unfortunately, I bounced off as I rode too fast around a curb. Luckily, I woke up before I hit the ground!

My real motorcycle adventure in Thailand mimicked the dream, minus the outfit of course! Once we had become settled in our home, the Peace Corps director, John, had discussed transportation with us. We would eventually need to travel to our work places and to our sons' nursery school. At the time, however, a Thai language tutor named Ajahn Buppha came to our house Monday through Friday mornings.

When John brought up the topic, I eagerly asked, "When do we get our car?"

"Car?" he replied with a puzzled frown. "I think bicycles would do nicely for now."

"Bicycles! But what about our sons? They're only four, so we can't leave them home! And wouldn't it be dangerous riding on the rutted dirt roads around our house?"

"Now, Pat!" John had a condescending note in his voice, which I found most irritating. "We'll have seats on the bikes for Mattie and Nate, of course. You know, Thai families do this all the time. Our goal is for you to live as much like them as possible."

Joe piped up. "Yes, Tricia, that's what we're supposed to do!"

What a traitor! I glared at him but realized I wouldn't get anywhere with this argument without his support. So we rode bikes.

Surprisingly, I didn't mind after all. Our little boys enjoyed riding behind us and we managed the dirt roads satisfactorily. We couldn't believe the variety of vehicles on the paved streets, though. Not only autos and bicycles, but taxis, trucks, buses, pedicabs, and motorcycles! Fortunately, traffic moved slowly. In Thailand, John told us, we needed to look only ahead, never to the back or to the side. Strange as it seemed, that advice actually worked well for us.

We felt closer to Thai people on bikes. Riding to the crowded market area, we could easily stop at a cafe for iced tea and snacks. People acted very eager to meet and talk to us. Often, of course, they asked for English lessons. We always refused this request, though, because we wanted to spend our free time as a family instead of teaching!

Our blond, blue-eyed, look-alike twins also drew crowds of people at first. While both boys loved the attention, we had to protect them from eager hands wanting to stroke their silky, yellow hair and pink and white skin.

Joe also came in for extra attention. Sitting in a cafe, with one arm flung casually on the chair back, he would feel a

Chapter 6
Motorcycle Mama

gentle touch. Looking around, he often surprised a Thai man lightly stroking the thick, curly, red hair that grew on his arms!

Soon it became time for us to start working, Joe at the Chiang Mai University biology department and me at the School for the Blind. Suddenly, John realized we needed faster vehicles.

"Now do we get our car?" I begged.

"Oh, no," John answered. "I think ... motorcycles—one for you and one for Joe!"

Hearing this, I blew up. "I just can't do it! I cannot, will not ride a motorcycle. And where would the kids ride? Perched on the back again? It's not safe!"

Can you guess that my husband supported John? Can you guess that I lost that battle too?

"Try it, Pat. Just try it out," they both urged.

Soon, a small motorcycle arrived at our door. Joe and John both showed me the basics—how to start and how to stop. Trembling with fear, I mounted the bike, started it, and slowly drove down our driveway, through the gate, and then turned right onto the dirt lane running past our house.

I practiced driving up and down the road for an hour or so. With great relief, I found I could manage the vehicle. The next morning, the boys left for nursery school driven by the kindly pedal cab driver across the street. I kissed them and waved goodbye, then anxiously propelled the bike to the blind school.

When the students heard the roar of the motorcycle, they rushed out of the classrooms. When they learned it was me on the bike, they crowded around, calling, "Mrs. Pat!

Mrs. Pat!" Most of them proceeded to explore the vehicle with their hands.

Needless to say, I felt vastly relieved. Maybe I could do this! I taught my lessons and then seated myself on the bike to drive home. Cautiously steering down the driveway and through the gate, I needed to turn right. My foot felt for the brake, first confidently, and then in panic—*where was it? Where was it? Oh no, I can't stop!* I tried to swerve, but I was traveling too fast. The motorcycle stalled and I found myself sailing over its top, landing on the dirt road with a perfect face plant.

After a couple of minutes on the ground, I slowly stood up, thankful that I had only a few scrapes. I got on the bike, found the brake, and drove home.

I walked into the house. Boon and my two little boys came running. Boon looked at me, her eyes widening with horror. "Mrs. Pat, what happened to your face?"

I walked upstairs to the bathroom and looked in the mirror. My right eye was swollen. A big bruise, rapidly turning purple and green, sat angrily on half my face. I called down the stairway, "Boon! I fell off that stinkin' motorbike!"

Mattie and Nate started to cry, so I rushed down the steps to soothe them. "It's okay, fellows, I'm okay. Pretty soon this big owie will go away, I promise!"

I tried again the next day, after putting on sunglasses to hide my black eye. First, though, I made sure that I could find the brake in any situation! Soon, driving it to school and back became almost second nature, although a flash of fear always accompanied me. I thought it kept me extra alert.

Chapter 6
Motorcycle Mama

Some evenings, after the boys had fallen asleep, Joe and I would pay Boon extra to babysit. Then we'd drive to the night market for a snack on his more powerful bike. We found it quite pleasant to motor instead of walking or getting a taxi. The streets proved well lighted and the traffic much less than during the day.

The night market featured an outdoor restaurant. I always ordered a Thai omelet, my favorite. Prepared in a huge wok, the filling was ground pork, large peas, and spices. The eggs came folded over the filling like an envelope.

Finally, I felt comfortable enough to venture taking Mattie and Nate to school. By then, we all had helmets. I asked, "Boys, would you like to ride to school with me?"

Very excited about the prospect, they exclaimed, "Yes, yes, Mommy, let's do it!"

We practiced first. Helmets on, we rode up and down the lane. I found that I could put one boy in front and one in back. It worked. My "fear factor" went into overtime, though. After all, I carried very precious cargo. At that point, I became truly amazed at the courage these little four-year-olds had shown since we had arrived. Our whole life there had become one great adventure for them, one they usually embraced wholeheartedly.

Then we experienced the Thai holiday of *Songkran*, the Thai New Year. Besides religious rites, the main feature of this holiday is throwing water on people to wish them luck during the coming year. It is held at the end of the dry season, when the weather is suffocatingly hot and a cool water bath isn't minded.

One day we took a taxi downtown and experienced it firsthand. We got soaked, but also threw water on others. The boys didn't like getting wet until we bought water pistols so they could fire back! Not only people, but vehicles got the water treatment too. To their chagrin, foreigners were blasted more than others. We noticed that Thais kept laughing no matter how wet they themselves became, so we copied their actions.

This holiday lasted for three days. We tried to stay home as much as possible, but one day, I returned home after running an errand. I traveled on the back roads in order to escape holiday revelers. But, suddenly, ahead of me stood six people lined up with buckets. I panicked. *Oh, my gosh! What am I going to do?*

Too late to turn around, I hunkered down and tried to blast through the group. Laughing uproariously, they soaked me. I lost control of the bike. It hit the dirt and I did too! As I struggled to right myself and my vehicle, these folks pointed and giggled at my distress. I could have cried. Instead, true to the spirit of the New Year's, I laughed and joked, "Ahh. I will have great luck in the months to come!"

Seeing their smug, smiling faces, a great truth hit me. *They really hate me! And why? Well, why not? I'm different—in looks, language, and lifestyle. I'm living in their country. And we have lots more money, two motorcycles, and servants. That list could go on and on. My neighbors smile and act friendly most of the year. But during Songkran, they have permission to show their true feelings—envy, resentment, and anger.*

Completely drenched, I gripped the motorcycle handles hard so they wouldn't see me shaking. Fortunately, my bike started on the first try. I blinked rapidly to chase the tears out of my eyes and rode home.

Recovering from this latest fall, I once again drove my bike without mishap. The fear that gripped me intensified. I kept on riding that bike, though, mostly because I felt hopeless that any change could be made.

Many months later, I started regaining my confidence. Then, one morning, as usual, I drove the boys to their nursery school. Arriving at our turn, I quickly eyeballed the oncoming traffic and swung left, but not soon enough. The young man coming toward us on a larger bike crashed into us with a resounding bang!

I picked up our motorcycle. Fortunately, traffic stopped while I wheeled it over to an empty lot close by and the boys walked alongside. Completely shaken, I thought, *What if Nate and Mattie are injured?* Our vulnerability hit me again. I heaved a great sigh when I examined them for injuries and they appeared okay.

"We're fine, Mom," they chorused.

Had I made a mistake? Not given myself enough room? Perhaps, but what happened next assured me this was no accident. The young man who hit me marched over. He and his bike looked perfectly fine. "You hit me!" he declared angrily. "Give me 500 baht or I will call the police!"

The baht was only worth five cents at that time, but still, 500 proved an enormous amount for most Thai people. I never carried that much money, but I sure didn't want the police involved. We had often been advised to avoid them at any cost! While I thought matters over, Mr. "Give me 500 baht or I'll call the police" kept repeating his demand in a low, menacing voice.

I looked in my purse, and then impulsively handed him the 50 baht I found inside. "Here's all I have," I told him.

He grabbed the bills, hopped on his motorcycle and drove away. That made me certain that he had speeded up and hit me deliberately in the hope of fleecing a foreigner, a not uncommon practice.

We continued our morning drive uneventfully. But the next day when we readied to leave, Mattie balked at riding up front. "Mommy, no! I can't do it!"

"Honey," I knelt down and spoke softly to him. "Are you afraid we'll have another accident?"

His little face contorted in fear. "Yes, yes."

"I don't blame you, dear. That was really very, very scary. Hmmmm. Well, we need to drive to school. Sooo, Nate, would you be willing to ride in front instead?"

"Sure, Mommy."

It did not take long for Mattie to eagerly assume the shotgun position in turn with his brother. Thank goodness, we didn't have any more accidents the rest of our time in Thailand.

What a relief it was to arrive back home in the good old United States of America! Traffic resembled the old Wild West in Thailand. In the U.S. regulations, such as speed limits, made me appreciate how vehicles flowed safely and smoothly most of the time.

Did I yearn for my little bike? Definitely not. In fact, arriving at our destination in Des Moines, Iowa, I turned to my husband and stated definitely, "The first thing I want to buy is a car!"

Chapter 7
Revolution

On October 14, 1973, after days of tension and demonstrations brought together over 400,000 Thai students and other residents of Bangkok, Thailand, violence finally erupted. They gathered to demand a new constitution and the release of fellow students held as political prisoners. By the time the violence ended the next day, nearly one hundred demonstrators lay dead. Several hundred were wounded by tank and machinegun fire. In response to the violence, the king (who is revered as a god in Thailand) met with student leaders, his prime minister, and the cabinet. In the end, the king crafted a compromise. Three top government officials left the country. The rector of Thammasat University became the prime minister, in charge of writing a new constitution. A new civilian government took over from the military dictators. The students won, but as one said, "We have made a new Thailand, but it cost us a lot."

After that day and night, to the jubilation of the Thai people, democracy had arrived—and we were there! That is, my husband, my two young children, and myself, huddled in a motel when the fighting began.

It had started a few days before. Our schools had recessed for holidays, so we decided to visit the big city for a few days from our home in Chiang Mai. Trips to Bangkok had proved enjoyable at other times, but I always felt a little on edge there. With few city regulations or services, we never knew what we might see. After once encountering a deserted dying woman and another time being frightened by a cobra on display, we always kept our guard up.

Boarding the Thai version of a Greyhound bus, we couldn't help noticing that the crowded vehicle contained an unusual number of university students. We recognized them by their tight, Western-style jeans and the boys' shoulder-length hair.

"Hmmm," my husband remarked casually, "seems like a lot of young people on the bus today."

"Well, they do have a week off," I replied.

While hoping for a stress-free visit, we had no idea of the momentous uprising that would play out around us. Peace Corps, for whom we worked, apparently hadn't known either. We received no warnings against traveling to Bangkok.

Arriving in Chiang Mai the year before, our director had told us, "This country is governed by a military dictatorship. Be very careful what you write home. Letters are usually opened and read before being sent. Any criticism may be cause for you to be deported."

While our day-to-day activities always proceeded smoothly, it proved unnerving to think that anything we wrote could be censored. You can believe that my parents received only

Chapter 7
Revolution

cheery weekly letters as I described for them the fascinating details of living in a different country and culture.

On our arrival during our break, Bangkok appeared peaceful. We took a cab to the Peace Corps office to check in and catch up on any news. Then we walked over to the motel where we always stayed. It proved to be clean and comfortable, with a swimming pool that thrilled our children. As a bonus, a restaurant with good, cheap food was available.

We ate lunch and settled into our room. Nate and Mattie changed into swim suits and swam in the pool, while Joe and I relaxed in deck chairs.

The next day we delighted in rambling around the part of Bangkok close to our motel. The city looked messy and dirty, submerged in a sizzling, humid heat. One didn't want to breathe in too deeply either, as a faint sewer smell often permeated the air. Nonetheless, it proved incredibly exciting. All kinds of shops crowded together. Stores and vendors sold everything imaginable: jewelry, furniture, cookware, clothing, and toys.

Food choices ranged from a few hotels serving Western food to restaurants with Chinese, Thai, or Indian dishes. Carts dotted the streets, each with its specialties, such as deep-fried bananas, chicken satay, or meatball noodle soup. As warned, we always ate cooked food, with one, glaring exception. Joe and I couldn't resist the spicy, tangy, green papaya salad. Perhaps the seasoning protected us because we never got sick.

Men from India, in their accustomed garb of turbans and floor-length robes, sold not only clothing, but also spices. Pleasing, often mysterious scents, wafted from the open barrels.

Joe's size proved especially useful, not only for carrying children, but also for crossing streets. It proved imperative to be seen! The traffic could provide unequivocal death traps for unwary pedestrians and riders alike. Every kind of vehicle, from buses to tuc-tucs, autos, taxis, pedicabs, motorcycles, and bicycles, speeded along. No helmets in sight, of course. And the huge loads balanced on some of those two-wheeled conveyances boggled the mind!

The next day, we planned to spend time in the open air market, acres of goods sold in colorful tents. Red, green, blue, and yellow flags often fluttered between the booths.

However, before we could leave, the motel owner rushed over looking quite agitated. "See TV in *rahn ahan*," (restaurant) he cried.

We hurried into the little cafe and ordered some breakfast. Our food grew cold as we gazed unbelievingly at the television. Yes, we had noticed groups of young people on the sidewalks the day before. Now these had grown to hordes and filled the streets. We watched in horror as soldiers and the police attacked them. Terror engulfed me even though I knew our motel lay a bit away from the uproar.

"Joe," I gasped, "what will happen to us—a foreign family in the city?"

"I imagine we'll be okay if we stay here," my husband decided. "Who knows how far this violence will go? And where? I don't think we should seek shelter in the Peace Corps office either. We might be attacked on the way there. Probably we are safer here than anywhere else."

Chapter 7
Revolution

I agreed. So we spent most of the day in the restaurant snacking, conversing with other patrons, and watching the bitter scenes play out on TV. We only left to go upstairs to bed in the evening.

All night the battle raged. While the rest of my family slept soundly, I tossed uneasily. Lying there in the dark, my imagination ran wild: *What would happen tomorrow? Would we survive? Or be sent home in body bags?*

After the dark hours, however, the sun rose. We dressed and hurried downstairs. The motel owner approached us, smiling happily.

"Is it over?" we asked with some trepidation.

"Yes, yes! Okay! Okay!" And he gave the thumbs up sign.

A tsunami of relief waved from my head to my toes! We all ate breakfast more heartily than usual. Afterwards, Joe prepared to ramble down the main streets again. I felt apprehensive, but we were assured again and again that everything was back to normal.

We heard that the king had arranged the truce. The dictators had left the country and a new constitution would be written. The students had won, and the government had become a democracy once again.

As we walked the boulevards, a sense of freedom pervaded the air. Smiling people crowded together, excitedly laughing and talking. The biggest proof that the old order had been overturned? Soldiers and the police, who had attacked the protestors, had disappeared.

In the middle of each intersection, instead of a law officer blowing a whistle and motioning traffic to go or stop, stood a—boy scout! These young lads, dressed in their light brown uniforms, stood perched on high platforms. They directed the flow of vehicles as efficiently as if they had done it all their lives.

The Thai people had answered a resounding "yes" to the siren call of liberty!

Chapter 8

The Goats of Wrath

My husband, our two little sons, and I had lived in Chiang Mai, Thailand, for about a year. Joe had responded to the cultural changes and his demanding position as a professor at the university by becoming quite irritable and morose. Unfortunately, he always felt someone or something else would make him happy.

One Friday afternoon, he walked in the door and wrapped his arms around me. "Tricia! I'm so happy! I just paid 100 baht for two goats!"

This didn't amount to a lot of money. However, I was absolutely stunned, to put it mildly. Joe had a PhD in zoology and had frequently brought animals home in the past. That is, until our own two little critters, the twins, arrived. They seemed quite enough.

I knew he loved goats. I always felt quite sure, however, that we'd never have goats at our home. Then and there, I resolved to put up a full-scale resistance. Nothing less would faze him!

All this flew through my mind as I pushed away from him. "Why? Why? Why?" I sputtered. "Where are they now? Where are you going to keep them? What will they eat? Won't they hurt our little boys?"

"Now, now," Joe remarked calmly. "We're going tomorrow to pick them up. I bought them from a farmer whose property is just off the superhighway. We've got a large yard with plenty of grass, Tricia. That's what they'll eat! Maa, our gardener, will probably be glad for the help. It's pretty tiring mowing grass with a scythe like he does!"

"No, no, no!"

"Tricia, it will be okay! You know, I don't like to pen animals up. As a zoologist, I like to observe their natural behavior. I'm sure they can roam around our yard. There's a high fence around our compound to keep them in. And if they wander over to the landlady's house or Murrie's place, I'm sure they'll just shoo them away. No problem!"

Hmmm. I didn't know about that. "But what about our boys, Joe?"

"Hey, Mattie and Nate! How would you like to learn to ride a goat? Just like your own little ponies! I bet we could even train them to pull a wagon you can ride."

The children, who had rushed over to see their daddy, cried, "Mommy! Mommy! Let's get the goats."

"I don't think so!" I broke in. "There's no way those creatures are coming here!"

"Tricia, I can just see myself now. I'd come home every day, call the goats over, and look into those funny barred eyes. Then I'd feed them and stroke them. It would be so relaxing for me, and you know how stressed I've been with teaching at the University and culture shock." He heaved a great sigh. "Tricia, I'd be so happy with goats!"

My parents had taught me that, in general, happiness comes from inside. I didn't think goats would help his mood that much. But—I felt myself weakening. "Okay, okay, but if they cause too much trouble, out they go!"

"Oh, of course, Tricia. Just wait, though. You and the boys will *love* them just as much as I do!"

Saturday afternoon Joe and I left the boys with Boon and walked down the dirt lane outside our home. As we headed for the superhighway, about a quarter-mile away, I asked more questions.

"Joe, did you tell the farmer why you wanted the goats?"

"Well, you know the Thai attitude toward pets."

Did I ever! Dogs in Thailand consisted of mangy, rabid scavengers. Cats needed to catch vermin for their keep. When I asked Boon what she fed our housecats, she replied, "*Muwos my tumyun, my gin ahahn layo!*" (If the cats don't work, they don't eat!) I insisted she feed them a little plate of fish scraps and rice every morning anyway. And even watchdogs didn't exist! If a wealthy person wanted his house guarded, he'd just hire a man to do it instead.

"So," I persisted, "what did you tell him, anyway?"

"I told him we planned to eat the goats," Joe answered.

We both laughed.

"Good idea!" I remarked. "If you had said you wanted them for pets, you'd really be considered a *farang moho!*" (Crazy foreigner!)

Arriving at the superhighway, we stood waiting for a tuc-tuc. These converted pick-up trucks roamed the streets of the city, being cheap, fast transportation. One only had to wait a few minutes for a ride.

A tuc-tuc painted royal blue stopped. The driver offered us a big smile. "*By nigh?*" (Where are you going?) he asked.

I told the driver, with my weird mixture that Boon called "Pat's language" that we wanted to ride to the farm down the highway to pick up some goats my husband had purchased.

His eyes widened; his mouth dropped open. Pointing to the inside of his vehicle, he asked, "Goats? Why?"

Rubbing my stomach, I replied, "*Gin a-hahn layo.*" (We will eat them.)

The driver grinned. Rubbing his stomach and glancing skyward, he muttered, "Mmmm! Goats *ahahn dee!*" (Goat meat is very good!) But I will charge you extra!"

Joe quickly agreed. "Okay, okay," he promised.

Arriving at the farm, the owner quickly walked up as soon as he saw us climb out of the tuc-tuc. He greeted us in traditional Thai fashion, by putting his palms together in front of his chest, bowing, and saying, "*So-wat-dee-crop!*" (Hello!) We returned the greeting in the same way, except we only inclined our heads. According to Thai custom, the higher the status, the less the bow. And, as a professor and a teacher, our status was sky-high.

The deal quickly concluded, and only one problem remained: getting the goats into the vehicle! The farmer tied ropes around the necks of each goat. I climbed in and cowered in the corner. Joe entered and held the ropes. While the driver watched, the farmer gave each goat a little push from the rear. They quickly scrambled up the steps into the truck. The two men laughed and exchanged rapid Thai with each other. No doubt, they said, "Aren't foreigners crazy?"

We rode right up to our door with the strange passengers. As the goats scrambled out, a crowd consisting of our servants and compound neighbors gathered.

Boon spoke first, in an agitated voice. "Ajahn Pat, why you bring goats home?"

I gave a shrug of my shoulders and pointed to my husband. "Ajahn Joe wants them, Boon! He wants to play with them."

Boon translated rapidly to the others. They shook their heads and uttered disbelieving grunts. Maa, our gardener, put his hands around his neck, indicating that the goats should be tied up.

"No, no!" Joe declared. "Goats *by tea, by tea!*" (I want the goats to roam around!) He matched the words with broad gestures of his arms. Then he pulled a few weeds, called the goats over, and sat feeding them and stroking their heads.

Everyone except Boon left, muttering to each other.

I tried to calm our cook. "If the goats cause trouble, Boon, Ajahn Joe is willing to get rid of them." Standing there with her hands on her hips, she threw me a skeptical glance. Then she quickly stomped back into the kitchen.

Oh, boy, I thought. *Now we've really done it—alienated our servants and the neighbors!* I hoped Joe proved right and the goats would cause no trouble.

The next day was Sunday. As usual, I walked outside to look around and enjoy the cooler morning air. Soon, I shrieked, "Joe! Joe! Come here right now!"

Joe ran outside. "What's wrong? Are the goats okay?"

"Okay?" I screamed. I pointed to three large pots, which had lately held three shrubs I was carefully nurturing. "Joe, those awful goats ate my plants up and just left a few sticks in each pot! You told me they ate grass! The grass isn't touched!"

"Oh, well," Joe answered calmly. "Tricia, those shrubs weren't doing well anyway. And you can always get more."

"I don't dare plant anymore. Your critters would just gobble them up!"

"Don't worry. I'll take care of them today. They won't get into any more trouble, I promise!"

On Monday, Joe and I left for work and the boys for nursery school. I prayed that our new pets would dutifully eat grass and stay in our yard.

Coming home at noon with Nate and Mattie, I found Boon standing by the front door tapping her foot. Trying to sound cheerful, I asked, "What's going on, Boon?"

"Ajahn Pat, goats go all over. Eat bush. Eat trees. Try go in my house!"

I closed my eyes for a moment, trying to calm down. "Oh, Boon, I'm so sorry! I'll speak to Ajahn Joe when he comes home. Surely he will get rid of the goats!"

But Joe adamantly refused. "Let them get used to their new home. I'm sure they will settle down!"

Tuesday, the boys came crying to me. "Mommy, we tried to climb up on the goats' backs, but they bucked us off!"

"Boys, don't go outside unless I am with you," I cautioned them after I made sure they were okay.

Joe heard another earful that afternoon. "I won't have my children tossed around and hurt by those creatures!" I insisted.

"Well, those goats just need training. Soon the boys will be able to ride them and play with them!"

On Wednesday, the boys and I had just strolled into the compound gate after a walk on the lane, when I heard Boon and See, Pun's replacement, screeching, "Ajahn Pat! Ajahn Pat!"

I ran into the house. "What is it?"

They both pointed upstairs. Barreling up the steps, I first looked into Mattie's bedroom. The frisky goats were jumping on top of his bed! One had even left a little pile on the coverlet.

I yelled, "Shoo, shoo, shoo!" as I herded them away. The three of us clattered down the steps. "Boon," I hollered, "open the door!"

When I had shut the door behind those critters, I looked up. See was bent double with laughter! Even Boon, whom I knew sympathized with me, smiled. I couldn't blame them. What a ludicrous sight we had made!

I sat down at the table and put my head on my arms for a couple of minutes. Then I wearily stood up, asking See, "Can you please help me now?"

The two of us went upstairs. See held the quilt while I cleaned up the goat pellets. Then we took the bedspread outside to soak in the big washing tub. "*Cop-coon-cah!*" (Thank you!) I told her and handed her a few extra baht.

You can imagine what Joe heard when he came home. It wasn't pleasant. However, all my passionate words still didn't faze him! "You make sure to tell the servants to keep the doors shut, Tricia!" After that I dreaded coming home! Should the boys and I stay in a hotel until Joe finally got rid of those creatures? *No*, I mused to myself. *I couldn't leave Boon alone with Joe and the goats.*

Thursday, I came home to find my cook once more with an angry look on her face. "Ajahn Pat! Goats go out gate, run down road, eat up flower garden! Man sell at market, now all gone!"

Oh boy. Now the neighbors outside our compound would be mad at us! When Joe arrived home, I told him what had happened. He spoke to our cook. "Boon, what were those flowers worth?" When she told him, he went to our locked money drawer and counted out enough for repayment, plus a little extra.

"That should do it!" he told her. "Now, Boon, make sure the compound gate stays closed so my goats don't get out!"

Friday, we sat eating dinner. Boon announced that a Thai man, Mr. Tan, had come to see us. We got up and exchanged traditional greetings, asked him to sit down, and offered him a drink.

"*Ow-arai?*" (What would you like?) Joe politely asked.

Boon listened to Mr. Tan. Her normally impassive face lit up with a huge smile. As soon as she translated, I almost cheered! Joe, however, looked stricken.

Mr. Tan had exclaimed, "I am here to buy your goats!"

Recovering, Joe replied, "Oh, I can't possibly sell them. I enjoy them too much!"

Nevertheless, Mr. Tan continued smiling and calmly repeated his request. Boon translated.

"But I enjoy those goats so much. Boys, don't you like the goats?"

Nate and Mattie proved no help. "Daddy, they butt us! We don't like them!"

Joe turned to me. "Tricia, you love those goats, don't you?"

"Are you kidding? I loathe those creatures!"

"Outnumbered at last, Joe addressed Boon. "Please ask Mr. Tan how much he will pay."

Mr. Tan smiled again. At last negotiations were going his way. "Fifty baht!"

"Oh, no, no! I paid 100 baht. I just can't sell them for half what I paid for them!"

At this point, Boon and I both threw Joe the nastiest, sternest looks we could muster.

His whole body slumped. "Okay," he uttered in a low voice. "I'll sell my goats for 50 baht."

"*By rao, rao*, Mr. Tan." (Take them away quickly!) I urged.

The new owner of the goats jumped up, pronounced, "*Cop-coon-crop*," (thank you) and quickly stepped out the door. Gazing outside, we saw him put a collar attached to a rope around each goat's neck and walk them out the gate.

Joe offered me a weary smile. "Well, that's a typical Thai solution. The neighbors probably got together and sent him to buy them. You know, they might have a goat barbeque. I understand that's quite tasty. But, really, Tricia, wouldn't it be awful if that happened to my goats?" He gave me a sorrowful glance.

Boy, I thought, *he is really bidding for sympathy.*

Now I knew the goats hadn't been the problem. It was Joe, with his fantasy those beasts could be treated like pets! Anyway, I had no love for the animals that had made my life miserable for the past week.

So I tossed my husband a saucy smile, patted my stomach, and said, "Yum!"

Chapter 9
Hijacked in Hong Kong

"Patricia, I've never seen anything like it!" my father gasped.

Chimed in my mother, "Dear, when you came down with chicken pox, you only had one little sore and missed just half a day of kindergarten."

It was 1974. My family and I had been on leave after spending two years in Thailand. Joe flew back after we spent a month visiting family in Iowa.

However, Mattie and Nate lay covered with sores from their scalps to in-between their toes and on the soles of their feet. The pox had even invaded the inside of their nostrils! So the boys and I could go nowhere.

I felt so fortunate that my parents helped me. My little boys cried and complained! Their itching proved severe, and my heart ached to see them suffer so. We smoothed Calamine lotion all over them and pulled gloves on their hands so they couldn't scratch the red bumps. Keeping active boys quiet proved quite a struggle, but after another month, they both healed without any scars.

Next we flew to join Joe. After checking our other bags, I lugged one carry-on, since we had an overnight stay in Hong

Kong. The kids each toted a metal Superman lunch box filled with small toys to amuse them on the journey.

First, we flew from Des Moines, Iowa, to San Francisco. There we boarded a Pan Am 747 jumbo jet and streaked nonstop to Tokyo. The flight stretched out interminably. Trying to keep two little boys amused all that time was a daunting task! Luckily, the huge plane even had space in the back where the boys could spread out their toys and play. A couple of other children joined them. Eating and sleeping rounded out those long hours. Back in the '70s, airlines still served full meals, drinks, and snacks.

After changing jets in Tokyo and spending more hours traveling, at last the plane landed in Hong Kong. Before our trip, the Peace Corps travel agent had soothed, "Don't worry, Mrs. Lidrich! An agent will be there to help arrange transportation to your hotel. Yes, it will be a modern one. First class. No worries! You and your little boys will be perfectly safe."

But we didn't land until late in the evening, around 10:00 p.m. Someone had miscalculated! Hustled through customs, I scanned the concourse. No one seemed in charge. In fact, all the offices and stores stood locked up tight. I later learned Hong Kong had an 11:00 p.m. curfew. And here we stood, in an alien place, completely abandoned. I could have broken down and cried. However, my little boys trustingly held my hands, so I stopped my tears.

Then the few people left in the airport quietly formed a circle around us. After two years in Thailand, I had come to expect this. My boys had pink cheeks, white-blond crew cuts, and light blue eyes. Even in the United States people would sometimes stare. But in Asia, my sons proved distinct novelties.

"Hello. We need—ta-xi! Ta-xi? Ta-xi?" I spoke slowly in English, but got no response. Then I tried the Thai language, to no avail.

Desperately, I assessed my situation. The kids and I drooped from exhaustion, but no one offered to help us. I saw no public phones, and what office would be open anyway? The group of people around us continued to stand quietly, staring. What should I do?

Then a little man pushed his way forward. Pointing first to me, then to himself, he spoke, "You! Me! Taxi!"

Unbelievable! He certainly didn't look official or like the transportation person from a prosperous first class hotel!

I replied, pointing first to him and then to myself and the children. "You! Take—us—to—hotel? Number one hotel?" He nodded emphatically.

What to do? What to do? Our only other choice appeared to be staying in the airport all night, an unpleasant prospect to say the least. But go with this man? To who knows where? What to do?

Finally, I just gave in and decided to go with him. An impromptu decision—like some others I have made and regretted in my life. *Please, God,* I prayed, *protect us in this strange place.*

The little man cheerfully smiled at the boys, then picked up my bag and led the way. A motorized pedicab stood in the parking area. "Is this your taxi?" I asked in astonishment.

"Oh, yes, yes!" he replied pleasantly. "You—get—in. We—go—fast! Fast!"

My sons climbed in eagerly. In Chiang Mai they had ridden a pedicab to nursery school, so it proved nothing new to them! After I settled in, the driver took his position on the bicycle and turned out onto the main highway. At that time of night, the empty road rolled ahead. A magnificent view encompassed thousands of city lights, like so many bright holes punched into a velvety black curtain. The air felt pleasantly warm, and a light breeze tickled our faces.

The boys curled up on each side of me, my arms around them. As they relaxed and cuddled closer, they made little contented murmurs: "Ooh, aah." Of course, they depended on me to keep them safe. But all the time my thoughts ran wild, *Where are we going? To a posh hotel or white slavery?* I shivered, not from cold, but from pure fright.

At last, our driver stopped in front of a small inn. *Oh no!* my mind shrieked. *This isn't my first class hotel!*

But a middle-aged woman ran out, smiling broadly. She knelt in front of my sons, staring in wonderment at those blue eyes and blond hair. Then she gently patted their shoulders. "She seems nice, Mom," Nate remarked.

Seeing the boys' drooping eyes and my drawn face, she didn't waste time. Motioning to the driver to take our suitcase, she escorted us to a clean, tidy room with three twin-sized beds. Then she asked, accompanying her words by the universal hand motions for eating, "You—hun-gry?"

"Yes, yes," I replied. Mattie grabbed her hand. "What do you have to eat?" he implored. "We're starved!" his brother added.

She laughed. "Sand-wiches?"

"Oh boy!" we all shouted.

Chapter 9
Hijacked in Hong Kong

What a relief! After being offered all kinds of food in Thailand, such as grasshopper curry, chicken intestine stir fry, and grilled ground wasps (minus the wings), American-style food would be most welcome!

In a few minutes, we sat munching chicken salad sandwiches with cold, weak tea to drink. I nodded approvingly to the woman when she brought in the jug of cold water colored light brown with tea to show the water had been boiled first, a necessity throughout the Far East.

After our meal, we prepared for bed. Since they had no exercise for that long day, the boys jumped fiercely on their beds for several minutes before they pronounced themselves ready to settle down and go to sleep. In spite of the noise they made, the innkeepers did not complain. Small children could do little wrong in that part of the world.

In the morning, our hosts smilingly waved goodbye. I offered money, but they shook their heads.

"So!" I mused. "*Maybe this is the first class hotel the Peace Corps reserved for us!*" Ah, well, I would never know. The driver whisked us to the airport and off we flew to Bangkok. But even though 40 years have gone by, I have never forgotten being "hijacked in Hong Kong".

Chapter 10
Thai Riverboat Adventure

In October 1974, we were finishing three years of service in the Peace Corps, stationed in Chiang Mai, Thailand.

An 18-year-old Lisu Hilltribe boy, Ophat Sanya, lived with us while he attended high school in the city. We inherited him from a couple of Peace Corps fellows who had finished their term and gone home. After living with Americans, his English proved quite good. Medium height and slim, he dressed in the standard schoolboy uniform of a white, short-sleeved shirt and knee-length blue pants. A crew cut topped his head, which was the norm for male students. His best feature proved his smile: two rows of even, sparkling, white teeth. Our whole family enjoyed Tee (Americans used "Tee" as a nickname for Ophat).

One afternoon my sons and I busied ourselves making simple, colorful toys together. Tee rushed into the room. "Mrs. Pat! Mrs. Pat! Would you, Ajahn Joe, and the boys like to travel farther north and go on a riverboat cruise? We'll be traveling up the Kok River, which is right between Burma (now Myanmar) and Thailand."

"I don't know, Tee. I understand that Burma is closed to foreigners and soldiers guard the borders."

"That's true, Mrs. Pat. In fact, my friends told me last year the Burmese soldiers used the riverboats for target practice. But—"

"Tee!" I interrupted hotly. "How could you even think we'd consider being Burmese bull's eyes?

"Mrs. Pat! It's okay! My friends told me this year everything is quiet."

"We'll talk to Ajahn Joe when he gets home, Tee."

As I had expected, my husband greeted the proposed trip with great excitement. I decided the boys and I could go too. Not only did the journey sound fun and interesting, but mostly I knew that Tee would take good care of us and keep us safe. A remarkable young man, Tee proved fluent in three languages (Lisu Hilltribe, Thai, and American English), and he understood each of the three cultures quite well. Since he had an engaging manner and acted very kindly toward my sons and myself, I had become quite fond of him. His parents had died, so he called me his *farong* (foreigner) mother.

We decided to leave at the end of the school term when we had a few days off. It was an ideal time weather-wise because then the dry season ended and the rain hadn't begun. On the appointed day, we packed our *yahms* (large cloth purses) and then Tee relayed us to the bus station on Joe's motorcycle. Finally, he locked the motorcycle at our house and grabbed a passing taxi, joining us just in time for departure.

"Look, boys," I pointed out as we boarded the bus. "See the white flower chains hanging from the rearview mirrors and the vase of blooms on the dashboard?"

Chapter 10
Thai Riverboat Adventure

Nate sniffed. "They smell really good!"

"Well, you'd never see a bus in the States decked out this way!" added Joe.

Tee remarked, "Thais love beauty, whether it's art, poetry, or music. Even their tonal language plays a tune!"

Villagers going home after a *teo* (pleasure trip) in the city made up most of the passengers. The men sported fresh-cropped hair and Western-style shirts and trousers. Some women dressed in blouses and slacks while others chose the common Thai outfit of a top and *pasin* (a long, wrap-around skirt). Bright colors abounded in the clothes worn, with orange and pink, or green and blue favorite combinations.

A few soldiers climbed abroad during the trip, as well as some university students and school children. The pupils were easily recognized by their blue and white, or black and white uniforms. By chance, we happened to be the only *farongs* (foreigners) aboard.

As the bus driver revved the engine, an old, toothless woman with a turban wound round her head stood and spoke urgently. The other passengers turned with an air of expectancy as she continued her plea. Just then, her husband and little granddaughter hopped on and the bus jolted forward.

Soon the smell of warm food drifted toward us from the bags and boxes of the other passengers, including our favorite curries and dumplings. Nate leaned toward me. "I'm really hungry, Mommy."

"*My-pen-lie*, son," (never mind) I answered as I smoothed his hair. "We'll be able to eat quite soon!"

One doesn't go hungry for long in Thailand. At each village stop, hordes of youngsters rushed over with tasty goodies that included fried chicken, dried beef, barbecued pork, and sticky rice wrapped in banana leaves. Drinks of iced tea, coffee, sugarcane juice, and coconut milk would be available too. These were poured into plastic bags and rubber-banded at the top with a straw sticking out. The food proved inexpensive too, as a quarter of a chicken might cost only twenty-five cents and drinks five cents each.

"It's surprising that we've rarely become sick from the food," I remarked. "Joe, you and I have become ill only once or twice. And the boys have eaten anything we've given them and never had a problem!"

"Well," Joe answered. "That's because we strictly adhere to the Peace Corps guidelines. He continued, as if reading from a rulebook, "Eat only cooked food, with the exception being raw fruit with a peel, such as mangoes, papayas, bananas, and pineapple."

I chimed in, "Yes, and drink only bottled beverages or drinks prepared from boiled water. It's better to skip the ice in restaurants or food stalls because it might be contaminated."

"Isn't it interesting," Joe pointed out, "how food servers show that the water is boiled by giving it a very slight tint of tea?"

As we drove along—up and down, mountain to valley—we noticed the intense, tropical sun highlighting the passing countryside.

"Look, kids!" I pointed out. "See the bright green of the half-grown rice in the fields? It practically carpets the area."

Chapter 10
Thai Riverboat Adventure

At intervals, we spied houses snuggled into clumps of coconut palms and banana trees. All were constructed of wood or bamboo and placed high on stilts. Being above ground kept homes clean and free from unwanted animal and insect life. In contrast, our own ground level house built in pseudo-Western style proved prey to all sorts of critters!

"Don't you wish we had a house built on stilts?" Joe asked.

"You bet!" I replied. "We wouldn't have troops of two-inch-long cockroaches storming the kitchen at night."

"Or the swarms of ants everywhere—under the staircases, in the corners, and anywhere a few food crumbs linger," Joe added. "You'd never guess that our maid mops the floors every day!"

"You know how Nate and I always clean up crumbs right away," spoke up Mattie. "Otherwise, the ants bite our legs. Ewww!"

"At least we haven't had snakes in the downstairs bathroom," Joe went on. "Boon warned us that they like the cool of the concrete floor."

"Yes," I responded. "Remember, she told us that they slither in through drainage holes, and they're practically invisible wrapped around the water jars. That is, invisible unless disturbed!"

We all paused a moment to silently count our blessings!

Just then, the bus driver pulled in to an open-air market for a short stop. Surprisingly, it contained only two or three merchants and a handful of customers. One woman sold plates of rice noodles with spicy curry and chunks of blood curd on top. Another offered deep-fried slices of banana and sweet potato from a huge black wok sizzling with hot pork fat.

Our ravenous sons ordered noodles and curry using enviably perfect northern Thai. As usual, people gathered around us. Their black eyes flickered with curiosity at the unusual sight of blond, blue-eyed twins who gestured and spoke exactly as natives!

Enjoying the spotlight, our kids spooned up their food and then fanned their mouths in exaggerated movements. "*Oh-ee, curry gang pet, gang pet!*" (Oh, the curry is very spicy!) they cried. Then those two imps dissolved in laughter, joined by their audience. The boys knew that a favorite national sport in Thailand is watching Westerners cope with hot peppers and spicy curries.

After our snack, we boarded the bus again but drove only a short way before we halted, this time for customs inspection. A policeman stepped on, quickly glancing at passengers and luggage.

"What're they looking for?" I whispered to Tee, while I trembled with fear. Thai police didn't exactly have sterling reputations.

"It's okay, Mrs. Pat," he soothed me quietly. "They constantly keep watch for jade and precious jewels smuggled in from Burma or China. Then, too, teak wood moved illegally from the north of Thailand, and opium in all its forms. They also search for bandits or Communist terrorists!" Fortunately, our bus passed inspection, and the policemen left.

Hearing a slight commotion behind us, we turned to see a young man and woman punching each other. She would reach over and punch him on the arm or leg, then sit back looking sweet and demure. Then it was his turn, and with laughter on each side, the game of courtship continued. Young couples couldn't touch romantically in public. However, punching was allowed, and signified love, not war.

Shortly, we arrived at Tathon, and the bus driver pulled right up to the river's edge. We hastily left the vehicle and strolled over to the bank. Looking across at Burma, Joe remarked, "Mysterious country! All locked up; nobody gets in and nobody gets out."

"It must be horrible to live in a virtual prison," I added.

Realty interrupted our musings in the form of our sons tugging on our shirttails with the announcement, "We're hungry, Mommy, Daddy! Can we eat now?"

I laughed. "Look over there, kids. There's a noodle soup stand just waiting for us!"

In no time we all crowded together at the rickety wooden table. Our meal, delicious as usual, contained pork meatballs. Factory-made, they always looked the same: uniformly round and grey in color. The year before, one of those manufacturers had been shut down for a while. The authorities had determined that the main ingredient wasn't pig, but dog!

This had caused great consternation. Not only because dogs proved the lowest form of life in Thailand—flea-bitten, rabies-scourged, scavenger mongrels—but also because of Thai religious beliefs.

The long-tailed motor boats, moored at the river bank, numbered seventy-two and regularly traveled between Tathon and Chiang Rai. Each craft looked like a large canoe with room for fifteen to twenty riders. Conveniently, we soon joined a parting group.

"Mrs. Pat," Tee whispered to me, "two dollars and fifty cents each for adults is fine, but the children should ride free."

When our turn came to go aboard, Tee declared to the boatmen, "You should not charge us for the boys." I spoke up in my fractured Thai, with appropriate gestures, "*Luc-fad mei, luc-fad mei.*" (The twins should be free.)

An argument ensued, but finally, the owners agreed, "Okay, okay." In Thailand, sellers and buyers always expected to bargain.

We climbed in and stashed our sandals in little wooden racks along the side. As we jostled for seats in the bottom of the boat, we assessed our fellow passengers. "Oh, look," I whispered to Joe, "we're in with a group of *farongs!*"

Surprisingly, they were mostly English and Australian tourists on a package jungle tour, while another young Australian studied Buddhist meditation at a *wat* (temple) a few kilometers down the river. Two Thai ladies, two Lahu Hilltribesmen, and a Buddhist monk completed the roster. Tee nodded toward one of the Lahu men, who sat contentedly puffing marijuana through a water pipe.

"See the army patch sewn on his jacket?" he whispered solemnly. "That's Burmese; he must be an army mercenary."

I gulped, noted that his rifle casually rested beside him and prayed for an uneventful trip.

Mattie and Nate shrank away from the *farong* tourists. That surprised me because the boys acted friendly to the many Westerners in Chiang Mai.

One Australian noticed the children's reaction and commented, "Your kids don't seem to like us very much. Don't they know any Western men?"

"Of course they do," I replied. Then I put my arm around Nate and pulled him close. "Honey," I asked him quietly, "do these men scare you? It's okay; they're very nice."

"Mom," he replied loudly, "they just have so much HAIR!"

The tourists laughed heartily, and we joined in.

"They aren't used to men wearing long hair and beards." I commented. "Western men working in Thailand cut their hair short like my husband does. Our nursery school teacher's husband has a beard, but it's trimmed close to his face."

Mattie and Nate couldn't be convinced that these fellows were harmless, though. They turned away and spoke rapidly to the Thais in the boat. Finally, settling down next to the Buddhist monk, they held his hands, cuddled close, and soon fell asleep. Obviously pleased with this attention, he patted them affectionately.

At mid-day, we sweated uncomfortably in the tropical sun. This was naptime at home, in the coolest spot one could find! Hats would have helped, but we had forgotten ours in the rush to leave. Fortunately, Tee shared his *pakima*, which, held over our heads, gave us some relief from the relentless heat. This strip of cloth is used by Thai men in several ways: maintaining modesty when bathing or lounging in the house, wrapped around the head as protection against the sun, or as a colorful belt. Looking over at our boys, I noticed with satisfaction that the monk had adjusted some of his voluminous robes so they were loosely covered.

"See the Hilltribe villages along the river?" Tee pointed out. "The Lahu, Lisu, and Karen tribes are located there." Tee, himself, belonged to the Lisus.

Looking farther in the distance at the mountains beyond, we spied an odd bald spot marring the lushness of the range. "That's another Lisu village about three hours walk from here," Tee explained. "The Hilltribe people cut and burn the trees and brush to make room for their houses and crops."

Tee further noted, "See those little green sprigs growing close to the river? There're opium poppies. The red, white, and pink blooms won't appear until December."

"Ah yes," Joe piped up. "This is part of the infamous Golden Triangle!" He went on, "We're in a triangular-shaped region comprising the northern parts of Thailand, Burma, and Laos. Here the Hilltribe people spread through the area illegally grow opium poppies. The wealth produced is enormous! So much so that any suppression has proved nearly impossible!"

An Australian man who had been listening spoke up. "If that's illegal, why doesn't the Thai government stop it?"

Tee laughed. "The Hilltribe men are very fierce," he explained. "Policemen have been found murdered near the villages. Now the authorities just raid heroin factories or opium caravans." He went on, "Even so, Thais have done everything they can to stop production of opium. The Hilltribe people have been made citizens and had medical clinics established for them.

"Our Peace Corps director told us that the Thai king has established agricultural programs to introduce crops other than opium," I stated. "Of course, the main problem is that opium is

Chapter 10
Thai Riverboat Adventure

such an easy crop to sell because the buyers go directly to the villages. Beans, on the other hand, have to be dried, shelled, and carted to market. A whole lot of trouble for them compared to opium! But it is hoped all these measures will encourage Hilltribe people to cooperate with the government."

As we talked, the boatmen headed for shore and pulled the boat up onto the muddy flats. Breaking out their round, metal lunch pails, they spread out a meal of sticky rice, a spicy curry sauce, and small steamed fish.

The curry was suspiciously bright green. Nonetheless, I dipped my ball of rice into it and tasted. The spices dominated so I didn't know what it contained. Tee ate some and then asked the boatmen, "What is the curry made of?"

At their answer, he started laughing and inquired of me, "Did you enjoy the grasshopper curry, Mrs. Pat?"

Oh, dear! My stomach churned a while, but I smiled at the boatmen and replied, "*Aloy muck!*" (It is very delicious!)

We had found that our neighbors in Chiang Mai ate certain insects. For one, a large beetle, which the woman next door told me proved delicious cut up in scrambled eggs! For another, a ground wasp. At certain times of the year, Thais poured boiling water into their nests. As the insects floated to the top, they were seized, stripped of their wings, and grilled. My children informed us they tasted very good. Sweet, in fact!

My husband, the zoologist, had explained to me that the meats and eggs so abundant in our country proved simply too expensive for people in much of the world. In Thailand, fish provided much of the needed protein, as well as very small amounts of beef, pork, and chicken. Insects filled in the gap!

As Joe had often remarked, "Protein is protein!"

The last two hours of the trip proved the most dangerous, since we encountered rapids several times. With clenched teeth, we huddled together as the churning, white foam drenched us and the boat rocked precariously. Each time, though, the skilled boatmen drove us through without mishap, their stolid faces revealing no fears. "Whew, thank goodness!" I sighed with relief when we had passed through.

We reached our destination, Chiang Rai, disembarked at the pier, and walked downtown. "Doesn't it feel good to stretch our legs after that long boat ride?" I remarked to the others. As usual, little children peeked at us and some followed, yelling, "*Farong! Farong!*"

When we reached downtown, we headed for a hotel. Tee left for the bus station, anxious to get back to Chiang Mai to study for a geometry test. Worriedly, he first inquired, "Are you sure you know your way home?"

We registered at the Siam Hotel and enjoyed its simple comforts. These included a room with two double beds, an electric overhead fan, and a tiled bathroom equipped with a cold-water shower and a squatting toilet.

When it came to showering, we had a lot of fun in the Thai bathroom. Tiles covered the entire room, even the ceiling! Bathing all together, we whooped, hollered, and tossed water all over each other! Somehow in the process, we managed to get clean. The extra water gurgled down a drainage hole in the floor.

Much refreshed, we headed for the hotel restaurant. The same tourists from the boat sat there, and we helped them order Thai food. What a spread! *Ky-yak-sigh* (omelets stuffed with pork and vegetables), *Khow phat* (fried rice), *doom-yam-goong* (dark red, spicy shrimp soup), fresh fried fish, and a huge quantity of boiled rice all graced our table. Although we were hungry, our friends proved especially voracious.

"You mustn't have eaten in a couple of days," Joe remarked.

"Indeed, that's actually true," one man replied. "We joined a jungle tour from Chiang Mai, and our leader actually starved us. Two biscuits for breakfast, usually, and the rest of the day only some food we couldn't eat cooked in the villages, like water buffalo fat curry." We shuddered and returned gratefully to the tasty meal in front of us.

We fell into bed early. In the morning, our kids bounced up at 5:00 a.m., eager for breakfast and a walk around town. We found the hotel restaurant closed at such an early hour, so we walked through town looking for an open cafe. The air felt refreshingly cool and pleasant; the streets were empty except for Buddhist monks begging their daily ration. Holding silver bowls, they swished by in saffron robes.

Spotting an open restaurant, the boys and I braced ourselves for a typical Thai breakfast of fish and rice. This meal had been the very first one our cook in Chiang Mai had prepared for us. As usual, Joe had gobbled it up, while I had picked at it, and our kids had adamantly refused to eat at all.

Now, tensing my stomach in the Chiang Rai cafe, I received the menu from the smiling waitress with trepidation. What a pleasant surprise! "Wow, boys, it's in English. And guess what? We can eat sausage, fried eggs, and toast!"

Mattie and Nate visibly relaxed, heaving big sighs. "Oh, great, Mom," Nate breathed.

The plates arrived colorfully decorated with tomatoes and green onions. We completed the meal with Ovaltine for the kids and *cafe rahn* (hot coffee with condensed milk) for Joe and me.

Tummies satisfactorily full, we caught the bus for home. We had experienced quite an adventure. What memories that trip evoked! As we rode home, my mind ran through some highlights: tasting grasshopper curry, shivering through the river's rapids, and discovering an English menu with Western food in a small, northern Thai town.

Most surely, I'd never encounter such wonders again. And I didn't think any other breakfast would ever taste so good!

Chapter 11
A Trip Back in Time

"Mommy, Tee's home!" Five-year-old Nate jumped up from the game we were playing and ran outside. Mattie followed in hot pursuit. They greeted the older boy with a torrent of Thai. Tee grinned and followed them into the house.

His eyes lit up now as he turned to me. "Mrs. Pat," he asked eagerly, "do you remember how much you enjoyed the riverboat trip we took several months ago?"

"Of course," I responded. "I loved it!"

Tee went on, "Would you and some friends like to come and visit my village soon? You know, my parents are dead, but my uncles, aunts, and cousins still live there and would like to meet you. I have told them about you, my *farong* mother, and how kind you are to me."

I blushed. "That's so nice of you, Tee! Actually, I'd really like to go, but I've only left the boys once for more than a day. When Ajahn Joe and I interviewed for the Peace Corps, they stayed with my parents so we didn't have to worry. But I'll tell you what. We can discuss this at dinner."

That evening, the proposed visit was our main topic of conversation. "My village is in a very beautiful area," Tee explained. "It is on top of a mountain, about three hours north of here."

My husband, Joe, ever one for a trip, talked excitedly. "You've got to go!" he enthused. "It's a unique opportunity, one you'll never have again in your life! Don't worry about the boys. I'll take care of them."

However, Mattie and Nate looked stricken. "You're leaving us? How long will you be gone?"

My heart fell, but all of us talked at once to reassure them. Joe promised to take them swimming, out to the *farong* restaurant for hot dogs, and maybe even to the small toy store in town. The children finally decided that my leaving would be okay if I came back!

I discussed the proposed plan with my friends. They were Anne, an English woman whose husband worked at Chiang Mai University; Barbara, another American Peace Corps volunteer; and Sarah, a Canadian Peace Corps volunteer. They eagerly agreed.

We decided to be gone three days, coming home on the morning of the fourth: one day to travel to the village and one to experience living there. The third day we would trek down the mountain and travel to a girls' school to spend the night. The morning of the fourth we'd come home. For luggage, each of us packed a shoulder bag made by Hilltribe women and decorated beautifully with exquisite embroidery. We each brought a little food, boiled water, a change of clothes, a small towel, soap, a toothbrush, and a comb. I had never packed so lightly in my life!

With hugs and kisses all around, I reluctantly left after Tee urged me, "Come on, Mrs. Pat! We do not want to miss the bus!"

We hurried down the *soy* (dirt road) to the superhighway. The Thais, by the way, had adapted a handful of American words, including "superhighway." Naturally, it had to be spoken in tones, like this: su-per-high-way.

A tuc-tuc came along, and the driver slowed and stopped. Leaning out the window, he beamed and asked, "*By nigh?*" (Where are you going?)

"*By* bus station," Tee replied, and the driver nodded and motioned us to board.

When we arrived, we spied Anne, Barbara, and Sarah, each with her packed shoulder bag similar to mine. They waved eagerly. Tee also spotted his cousin Alak, who planned to accompany us.

The four of us women wore comfortable, casual clothes that adhered to Thai modesty standards: short-sleeved tunics machine-embroidered on the necks, sleeves, and around the hem, along with long, cotton pants.

"I can't believe we're actually climbing a mountain and visiting Tee's relatives!" Anne enthused. The other women nodded, all agreeing this would be an unusual adventure.

Our bus proved old and creaky, sported more than a few dents, and needed a paint job. The seats inside were covered with cracked, worn vinyl. Its condition didn't matter at all. Our minds were focused on our destination.

After a couple of hours of traveling farther north, we arrived at a small village where Thai passengers waited for a tuc-tuc. We joined the queue, and as soon as one came along, we pushed in with the others. All of us packed in tightly, probably six to a side.

Shortly, an unbelievably foul odor wafted around the vehicle. I knew that Thais kept scrupulously clean. It couldn't be them! While Hilltribers bathed only right before their New Year, fortunately, Tee and his cousin had adopted Thai cleanliness standards. So it wouldn't be them!

Oh no, I thought. *Is it me?* Surreptitiously, I quickly sniffed each armpit and then gave a sigh of relief. Not me! I turned my head right, then left, inconspicuously sniffing the people sitting on either side. Not them either! Who, or what, could it be?

Shortly, the tuc-tuc stopped at another small village. A lone woman stood up, reached under her seat, and pulled out a huge bag, packed full!

"*Ow-arai?*" (What is in your bag?) I asked politely.

She grinned, showing a gold tooth in front. "*Gang-pet-bpla,*" (fish to prepare spicy curry paste) she answered.

Mounds of curries labeled red, green, yellow, or Massaman were sold in the markets. I knew the base of these delicious spicy pastes was fish, but rotten fish?

I smiled back. "*Dee-muck,*" (very good) I answered politely as she walked off the bus. *Yuck! Will I ever eat curry again?* I asked myself.

After bouncing up and down on the hard, wooden seats, we finally reached our destination. Tee grinned. "We get off here, Mrs. Pat. There is the trail which leads up the mountain."

At the trailhead a short, muscular Hilltribe man waited for us. Dressed in his everyday clothes, he wore voluminous, baggy pants ending below the knee, a wide belt, and a loose vest, all in black, handwoven cloth. A rifle dangled over his shoulder. Tee greeted him affectionately, then turned and introduced him. "This is my uncle! He is going with us to our village."

My friends and I all nodded and smiled at Uncle. "*Sowat-dee-cah,*" (hello), we chorused, as we made the traditional Thai greeting by pressing our hands together at chest level and giving a small bow. We couldn't speak the Lisu language but figured he probably knew a little Thai.

I motioned Tee to come close and whispered, "Why does he have his rifle with him?"

He gave an embarrassed laugh. "Well, Mrs. Pat, sometimes this mountain can be a little dangerous. There could be wild animals or thieves looking for opium." At my startled expression, he soothed, "But I'm sure we will be safe."

Clearly anxious to go, Uncle grunted and pointed his arm forward, so we started up the path. Jungle surrounded us, but we didn't worry. Uncle toted a gun! We laughed and talked as we headed ever upward.

At first it was fun, but then the hours passed and the climb grew tedious. We walked slower and slower. One time we passed two pretty Lisu teenage girls running down the mountain. Dressed in their best, their black, knee-length tunics sported colorful embroidery of red, blue, and green. Their trousers, also black, stopped just below the knee. A wide, black belt held the outfit together. Flat, pancake shaped hats with colorful streamers sat on their heads. As they hurried down the mountain, giggling and chatting, the streamers bobbled in time with their steps.

Any time we asked for a rest, Uncle would glance heavenward and shake his head slightly, because he climbed without difficulty. His massive chest revealed someone with great lung power and stamina, probably gained from frequently traipsing up and down the mountain.

Suddenly, Tee whispered, "Stop!" Fearing the worst, we halted, trembling. But Tee smiled and pointed upward. On a tree branch above us sat a great hornbill bird. We watched, fascinated, keeping as quiet as could be. I recognized the large, downturned bright yellow beak. Tee once had brought two hornbill heads home, one each for Mattie and Nate.

"How imposing," Barbara breathed, as we gazed past the beak to its curious, crooked, bright yellow neck and the sleek, black body with white tail feathers.

"Yes," Tee replied, "and very good to eat!"

At one point, the forest cleared, and the path ran by a swiftly moving, shallow stream. A Lisu man stood in the middle. While Uncle was outfitted for everyday, this man wore a loose-fitting, double-breasted, long-sleeved tunic, along with baggy pants and a wide belt. His embroidered shirt sported many rows of handcrafted, shell-shaped silver jewelry, stitched to the front and back.

We stopped for a break, and the Hilltribe men exchanged greetings. Tee reported to us, "He's all dressed up for the New Year." Then, giving us a wicked grin, he added, "Once a year he treats himself to a bath!"

It grew dark, and I could hardly place one foot in front of the other. Then I spotted a wooden bench in a small clearing off to the right side of the path. "Tee! Can't I just sleep here tonight? You can come and get me in the morning!"

"Oh, no, no, no, Mrs. Pat. You know, there are tigers here at night, and one might eat you! It really is not much farther."

All of a sudden, I experienced a great burst of energy. "Okay, okay, Tee! I sure don't want to be a tiger's dinner!"

About a quarter-mile more, we came into a large clearing. The bonfire in the middle illuminated several people gathered round, while in the background stood their homes. We had arrived! And—I felt ready to drop.

Knowing we felt very tired, Tee introduced us quickly to the group. One of the ladies led us to our quarters. A simple bamboo hut, it had a thatched roof and a dirt floor. Villagers had made it comfortable by laying down blankets for us to sleep on.

In a few minutes, two more ladies came with hot tea and bowls of rice mixed with herbs and roots from the jungle. Thank goodness, wooden spoons sat on top of the rice. We wouldn't have to wrestle with chopsticks! Not realizing how hungry we had become, we gobbled up our dinner. Our own provisions had been shared with Tee and Alak on the way up, while Uncle had refrained from eating.

Before Tee left, he turned to me and confessed, "You know, Mrs. Pat, there really are not any tigers out there. But I could not leave you in the jungle all by yourself."

"That's okay, Tee," I replied. "The thought of an attacking tiger spurred me on!"

Lying on the blankets in our clothes, we chatted softly. Outside we heard Tee, Alak, and some other boys calling out to each other as they splashed in a stream. With this soothing accompaniment, we dropped off to sleep.

The next morning we awakened at first light. Tee stood outside and whispered to me, "Mrs. Pat! Are you awake?"

"Yes, yes!" we all answered. Tee and the same ladies from the night before came in with more hot tea and bowls of rice.

Tapping the arm of the woman closest to him, Tee introduced us. "Mrs. Pat, this is my aunt, who raised me after my parents died." He spoke to her in the Lisu language then translated for me. "I told her that you are my *farong* mother and have been very kind to me."

I gestured the Thai greeting, saying, "*So-wat-dee-cah.*" Her face split with a wide grin, which proved a little disconcerting because she had so few teeth left! Tee translated her words. "She says she is so happy to meet you. She worries about me living in Chiang Mai and is glad I am living with your family."

"He is a very good son," I addressed her. "He is obedient, studies well in school, and entertains my little boys." One mother to another, we gazed in each other's eyes for a few moments.

"When you all have finished eating," Tee informed us, "I will be outside, and we can tour the village."

After we had eaten breakfast, we attempted to freshen up a bit. We couldn't bathe, but at least each of us had a little boiled water left in our packs, so we could splash a bit on our faces and scrub our teeth. Our change of clothes would be saved for the journey home.

"Oh well," Anne shrugged, "we're far from clean, but from what I've seen, we fit right in with the villagers. Especially if they only bathe once a year!"

Stepping outside, we oohed and aahed over the magnificent view! A plateau formed the mountaintop. Looking down, we could see for miles. Dense jungle gave way to the green and brown squares of the cultivated fields in the valley below. In some other places, trails led up to even higher mountains.

"We're standing on the roof of the world!" Barbara cried. We all nodded in agreement, overcome by the beauty around us.

"Where's your swimming hole, Tee?" Sarah asked.

He chuckled. "Turn around! Lisus are the engineers of all the Hilltribers." A stream flowed on one side of the village. It had been dammed up and a bamboo pipe thrust into the dirt wall. A stream of water flowed out of the pipe into a large pool below.

As we walked with Tee, we basked in the cooler air. Such a relief after being smothered by the steamy tropical heat below! A few villagers approached and Tee introduced us. Everyone acted polite and friendly. "People aren't shy here," Anne remarked.

"Lisus are the most outgoing of all the Hilltribe people," Tee responded proudly.

A woman pointed to a small girl standing nearby. Angry, red scars covered one side of her face, and her right arm hung down, useless. Tee translated the woman's words. "Her daughter fell into the fire a few months ago. What can she do to make her better?"

Oh dear. We looked at each other puzzled. We had no medical training. However, these people apparently thought we knew everything! What could we say?

"Tee, tell her to take her little girl to the medical clinic," Barbara suggested. Tee interpreted, and the woman smiled and nodded as we walked on.

At a hut toward the end of the village, Tee stopped. "One of our grandmothers would like to meet you."

Bending our heads, we entered the dim interior. Sitting upright on a pile of blankets, a sturdy, elderly woman stared at us. Like everyone else in the village, she dressed in a simple tunic and below-knee–length trousers, both made from coarse, homespun black cloth. Her gray hair stuck out from her head in untidy clumps.

Despite her poor garb and simple living quarters, her face radiated contentment and good humor. Peering at her intently, I suddenly realized why. From her chin to the corner of her eyes, the wrinkles on her face all angled up! *How wonderful.* I mused to myself, *Here sits a happy woman.* Just looking at her tempted me to smile.

Tee spoke to her and then translated. "Grandmother says she is eighty-five years old. While she can still walk up and down the mountains, she now gets a little tired. What can she take for more energy?"

The four of us conferred. "Can you imagine?" Sarah asked.

"Most Americans in their eighties can hardly walk, let alone climb hills!" I exclaimed.

Anne turned to Grandmother, who listened eagerly. "You might try putting a little sugar in your tea," she suggested.

Tee translated, and the woman beamed. The smile, which illuminated her whole face, proved contagious. Laughing and waving goodbye, we exited her home, still shaking our heads in astonishment at her good health.

Strolling through the village, we left the homes behind and arrived at a large garden plot. I recognized the beans, but in-between their rows stood lines of dry stalks—plants I had never seen. Each stem had a bulbous seed head on top.

"Tee," I asked, pointing to the strange plants. "What's growing here?"

Tee gave us an embarrassed smile and then looked down at the ground. "Opium," he whispered.

"What are those vertical slashes on each pod?" Anne asked.

"The opium sap is collected that way," Tee answered. "Those cuts are made when the pods are green. The juice is left to harden and then scraped off."

"Ohhh," we all murmured. Tee didn't need to say anymore. We already knew about the cultivation of opium in these villages.

Our Peace Corps director, John, had informed Joe and me, "Hilltribe people have grown opium since the 1920s. In fact, the Golden Triangle, comprised of northern Thailand, northeast Burma, and northern Laos, has been one of the top producers in the world."

He continued, "The king of Thailand has been trying to eliminate the cultivation of opium. First, they tried suppression, sending Thai police to the villages to destroy the crops. But the Hilltribe men are fierce fighters. After they killed a few of the lawmen, the Thai government hired agriculture agents from the UN. Along with Thai agronomists, they have been teaching the Hilltribers how to grow other crops."

Anne asked, "Do your villagers use opium themselves?"

Tee scowled. "Not many," he replied gruffly. "It is used mostly for pain relief when someone is sick or old. If anyone gets addicted, he is thrown out of the village and has to live somewhere else. In fact, there are a few villages made up entirely of opium addicts!"

The delicious aroma of roasting meat drifted over, interrupting our conversation and reminding us how hungry we had become!

"What's cooking, Tee?"

"Mrs. Pat, since you are my *farong* mother and have been very good to me, we are cooking a pig for you and your friends."

"Oh my gosh, Tee!" I replied. "That *is* a great honor. I don't deserve it, though. It has been so easy having you live with us. But thank you, thank you so much! Tell everyone we greatly appreciate it."

Frankly, though, I felt deeply torn. These people ate rice most of the time. If they did have meat, it might be any game they could find in the jungle, even birds or snakes. Pigs, no doubt, were either trundled to market for cash or eaten only on very special occasions.

But, on the other hand, I couldn't refuse such a great tribute. Indigenous people, I knew, would go to great lengths to be hospitable and quite insulted if someone did not accept.

That evening, we gathered in our hut, the four of us, Tee and Alak, and Tee's aunt and uncle. Village women passed bowls of steaming pork stew around, along with cups of hot tea. My bowl had vegetables, yes, but also extra pieces of pork piled on top until the dish almost overflowed. My perks as the honored guest!

My friends and I raved about our food. "Tee, tell them how good this is and how much we appreciate it. The pork is very tender, and I have never eaten such delicious vegetables," I told Tee, who translated. Everyone beamed.

To tell the truth, I liked plant foods much more than meat and wondered to myself whether the vegetables came from the woods or the cultivated fields. I made sure, though, to choke down every last piece of pork, lest anyone be insulted!

The next morning, after a breakfast of rice and tea, we thanked the villagers again and waited for Tee, Alak, and Uncle to guide us down the mountain. We had decided not to wear our clean clothes yet, since we planned to stay overnight at a girls' school before heading home.

The descent proved easy; in fact, we almost ran! Halfway down, though, I tripped on a root, fell, and bloodied my knee. In a couple of days, this injury became infected in the moist heat of the lowlands. When it finally healed, it left a scar that stayed for many years.

Reaching the base of the mountain, Uncle started back up. The rest of us caught a tuc-tuc bound for a nearby town. When we reached it, we headed on foot for the girls' school, while the boys traveled back to Chiang Mai.

By the time we arrived, the sun was setting. We had become so grungy on our trip that we longed for cool baths and clean clothes.

The headmistress greeted us enthusiastically, bowing deeply. "*So-wat-dee-cah!* We are honored to have you grace us with your presence. The girls have been looking forward to meeting you! You must be hungry. Come! We have prepared a banquet, and the girls will sing."

"We looked at each other, worry in our eyes. Thai people always, always kept themselves immaculate. And here we stood, wrinkled, dirty, and probably stinky. Spots of blood stained my trousers.

Barbara, who had arranged the visit, asked softly, "Would it be possible for us to bathe and put on clean clothes first?"

"But we are ready to eat," the headmistress argued. "Come! Nobody cares what you look like."

Miserably, we slunk inside. There stood about sixty female students, all dressed in white blouses and blue skirts, and all as pristine as could be!

They bowed, chorused, "*So-wat-dee-cah,*" and clapped. One of the students came forward and showed us to our seats. Tables stood piled high with delicious smelling delicacies.

Our hosts, like all Thais, treated us with the utmost courtesy and respect. Unfortunately, we were so tired and dirty that it proved a most uncomfortable evening that seemed to drag on and on. First, we heard the welcoming speeches in English. After that we ate and then listened politely as the girls sang.

My face stiffened from smiling and repeating, "*Cop-coon-cahhh.*" (Thank you.) At last it was over and my friends and I tiredly dragged ourselves to our rooms. We requested a bath before bed and, fortunately, they agreed.

Early the next morning, we left after a tasty breakfast of Thai rice soup with tiny dried shrimp and herbs added.

Reversing our route, we took a tuc-tuc to a nearby village where we could catch the bus for Chiang Mai.

In the early afternoon, I walked down the dirt lane and through the high gates that guarded our driveway. Two little "rockets" blasted out of the house. Mattie and Nate almost knocked me down, smothering me with hugs and kisses.

"You came back!" shouted Mattie.

"We missed you!" breathed Nate.

I could see my husband and Boon standing in the doorway, both smiling and waving.

Tee strolled over. "Did you have a good time at my village, Mrs. Pat?

"I loved it, Tee. Every minute! It's such a beautiful place, and the people are so kind. But," I continued, as the boys wound their arms around my waist, "it's awfully good to come home."

Chapter 12
Remembrances

In May of 1975, my family and I finally arrived home from Thailand. I had suffered bouts of intense homesickness all during our three years there. It proved wonderful to be among my relatives and friends again. Although I knew several Westerners who loved the Far East and spent year after year there, I felt like an American through and through. But were we completely home again? We soon found out.

A drive to the mall came first on our agenda. Such an American thing to do! But the strangest thing happened.

"Do you feel all right?" I asked Joe.

"What do you mean?"

"Well, it's so terribly loud here. Everyone is talking and it just grates on my ears! Not only that, but the buildings look so high. And Americans are huge!"

"I feel the same. Do you want to go home now?

"Yes—back to our peaceful little town!"

"You know what's wrong, Tricia? Reverse culture shock!"

True. Because of the vast differences in culture and climate, it had taken us a long time to get used to living in

Thailand. Now the process was being reversed! That made me think of our first weeks in Chiang Mai.

On a trip to the downtown market there, we had felt suffocated by the crowds of people, although we towered over most of them. The area was filled with stalls covered by large umbrellas or tent coverings. Our eyes ogled every kind of foodstuff available. Some tables held mounds of curry paste and others bloody piles of beef or pork. Plucked chickens with heads and feet attached hung from hooks. Seafood of every kind garnered attention. Fruit and vegetables lay stacked neatly on other counters, some completely unknown to us.

"Wooo! See those long beans!" Nate had exclaimed.

"Yuck!" Mattie had shouted. "Those fish're lookin' at me!"

Suddenly, I had turned to Joe and asked, "Do you notice anything in particular? I mean, other than all the strange foods here."

"Yeah. It's so quiet compared to home."

True. The market had been crowded, but the Thai language's music had flowed around us. Sometimes the jarring notes of English or German had interrupted, but mostly, we could imagine strolling through a symphony.

"Notice anything else?" I had persisted.

When Joe had shaken his head, I had nodded to the cash registers. "Look! Every person taking money is a woman! And I thought ladies would be sort of downtrodden here."

He had laughed. "Not really. You know my department head at the University is a woman. And several of the teachers are females."

I had replied, "Yes, and we have a lady dentist, Dr. Dang."

Chapter 12
Remembrances

"Remember when we went to the bank? We walked in to open an account, and the five teller cages stood manned by young men. However, they all passed money back and forth to an older lady sitting at a desk behind them."

That had recalled our Peace Corps director John's cultural lesson: "You know, even though this is 1972, women's lib doesn't seem to have made much of a dent yet in America. Here, though, in a so-called Third World country, women are prominent in professions and business. As far as money is concerned, men are considered butterflies, so women are the managers at work and at home.

"Yes," he had concluded, "men may have more social liberties, like being able to have more than one wife or take a mistress, if they can afford it, or visit prostitutes with their friends. But guess who decides how much fun they want their husbands to have and gives them an allowance? The wives!" John's revelations had dumbfounded us. Customs permissible in Thailand might mean criminal action at home.

"Remember when we tried to pay our bill at the dentist, Joe?" I had asked.

"Right!" We had knocked on the door, and a well-dressed young man had answered. The dentist wasn't in. When we had asked if we could give the money to him, he had laughed.

"No, no. Wait 'til she's back. I'd just spend it!" Butterfly, for sure!

After we returned to the States, in the weeks, months, and years ahead, we reminisced about the fascinating parts of our experience. Observing the beauty of the temples, for example, with tiled dragons crouched at each entrance. Watching monks dressed in saffron-colored robes stroll through the streets at dawn, their begging bowls held before them. Seeing delicate, silk-costumed teenage girls dancing ancient Thai steps. Traveling to a logging area and observing elephants carrying logs and stacking them.

Of course, frustrations abounded. Living in a tropical climate proved enervating for us. Fortunately, Chiang Mai stood located in the northern mountains. For about three months in the winter the temperature cooled down considerably.

Learning the language proved trying because we had to remember not only the words, but the tune! Joe could never do this because he had no ear for music. His Thai sounded like a bunch of silverware clanking together. As a result, I often heard, "Tricia, would you speak for me?"

Absorbing cultural nuances proved almost as difficult. We remembered Ajahn Buppha, our diligent Thai tutor, and her warnings. "Don't eat walking down the street. It's very rude. When you motion a Thai to come to you, you must keep your palm down. Palm up, the way you Americans do, is to call an animal. That is almost unforgivable! And never, ever put your feet up so the soles face another person." She repeated those rules so much that I have never forgotten them.

Class differences became extremely important there also. One day Boon said to me, "Mrs. Pat, which twin is older?"

Without thinking, I replied, "Nate, by five minutes."

Later, I spoke sternly to Boon, "Everyone is telling Mattie he needs to give in to Nate all the time. This is not an American custom, Boon. You must not do that anymore!"

Chapter 12
Remembrances

However, Boon didn't want to change. I sighed to Joe, "Everyone is telling Mattie he must kowtow to Nate! And Mattie is so angry!"

Together, we told Boon that we had been wrong. That we actually did not know which boy was the elder. The Thais had become confused and had stopped that objectionable behavior.

No matter the frustrations, though, we always retained a fondness for Thailand. We loved the food, especially after Boon learned to turn out one tasty dish after another. Eating out also proved a popular Thai pastime.

In the hot month of May, the mangoes ripened. Then we headed for a restaurant to eat the fresh fruit served with sticky rice. Evenings at the night market, I always ordered the Thai omelet. Cooked in a two-foot-wide wok, stuffed with ground pork, peas, and seasonings, it tasted scrumptious.

Invariably, people in Thailand acted polite and friendly. They also encouraged us when we tried to speak their language. The first word I learned was *dee*, meaning "good."

One day in the market, I spouted *dee* about everything I saw. Invariably, the Thai merchant would grin and answer, "*Oo—poot Thai ging muck!*" (You speak Thai very well.)

A phrase we usually did not like to hear, however, was *my-pen-lie* (never mind). Spoken by a Thai, it often meant that something we wanted done right away might be accomplished at a later time—or never. Joe and I would say to each other, "If I hear *my-pen-lie* one more time!" Of course, Thais would smile and laugh and then all would be forgotten until the next incident.

For me, our years in Thailand proved bittersweet. Pleasant people, delicious food, but the culture proved too different from my own. I didn't want my sons growing up in such a stratified society. I felt appalled at the relationship between Thai husbands and wives. The grinding, unreachable poverty was heartbreaking. But most of all, I missed my family and didn't want Nate and Mattie to forget them.

Anyway, because of our very different appearance, we could not really fit into Thai society. For example, back then, only Thai citizens could own property, and foreigners could never become citizens.

The people I felt sorriest for were the sons and daughters of American missionaries. These children had grown up in Thailand and acted and thought like Thais, not Americans.

This reminded me of a conversation I had with the boys' kindergarten teacher, the daughter of American missionaries. With her soft-spoken words and native gestures and mannerisms, she appeared to be Thai except for her pale, freckled complexion and strawberry-blonde hair!

Anna told me, "I've just come back from college in the States. You know, I'm so happy to be home. I didn't like it at all. I never want to go back there to live."

Poor Anna, I mused to myself. *Thai on the inside, American outside. Try as much as she can, she can never really belong here.*

At least our time there allowed me to find that I am most certainly 100% American and glad of it. Living in a very different culture actually helped me appreciate my own more. However, the three years I spent there have marked me.

For instance, certain Thai words express my feelings better than American words. To me, *si-bye dee* (very comfortable); *rao, rao* (go fast); and *ri-ep roy* (very correct) all improve on their English translations!

Certainly, I am "made in America," but also "tempered" in Thailand.

Pat with cook Boon outside of Chiang Mai home.

University of Chiang Mai where Joe taught in the biology department.

An elephant festival in Chiang Mai.

The Goats of Wrath and Other Stories
A Peace Corps Family's Adventures in Thailand, 1972–1975

Mattie sits on the steps to a small chapel. The pictures on the doors depict the epic tales of Thailand.

Mattie and Nate at Bangkok Zoo, feeding the giraffes long beans.

It's cold! Pat outside of Chiang Mai house. In January, temperatures could go down to freezing.

Boys playing outside toy store in Bangkok.

Boys looking at wares of seafood vendor in Hua Hin, Thailand.

Hilltribe woman in her native costume.

Pat attending Thai wedding.

About the Author

Teaching Thai blind students to speak English gave Pat a unique experience for which she is grateful. She went on to teach elementary and special education students for a total of 32 years, retiring in 2002.

Pat and her husband, Neal Haines, live in Oregon. They love the scenic areas of their state, and for many years hiked and cross-country skied in the mountains.

Her interests are varied. She enjoys being with family and friends and is active in her church. She has been a yoga and meditation practitioner for the last 30 years. An avid reader, historical novels and mysteries are her favorites. In addition, Pat writes on a variety of subjects, including politics and life experiences. Western Oregon has a long growing season, and she and her husband garden from early spring to late fall.

CPSIA information can be obtained
at www.ICGtesting.com
Printed in the USA
FFOW04n1244230417
34778FF